THE ILLUSTRATED ENCYCLOPEDIA OF *BOATING*

Alan Lucas

CHARLES SCRIBNER'S SONS
New York

Copyright © 1977 Alan Lucas

Library of Congress Cataloging in Publication Data

Lucas, Alan.
   The illustrated encyclopedia of boating.

   Originally published in 1977 under title: The
complete illustrated encyclopedia of boating.
   1. Boats and boating—Dictionaries.   2. Yachts and
yachting—Dictionaries.   I. Title.
GV775.L8   1978   797.1'03   78-9809
ISBN 0-684-15900-7

1 3 5 7 9 11 13 15 17 19 V/C 20 18 16 14 12 10 8 6 4 2

Printed in the United States of America

Contents

PHOTOGRAPHS

Scattered throughout this book are a miscellany of photographs to support the countless relative illustrations. They will be found on the following pages:

ILLUSTRATIONS.

Every term requiring illustrative description will be found close to the text. These number in their thousands. Extra illustrations which are as much general interest as they are directly related to text will be found on the following pages:

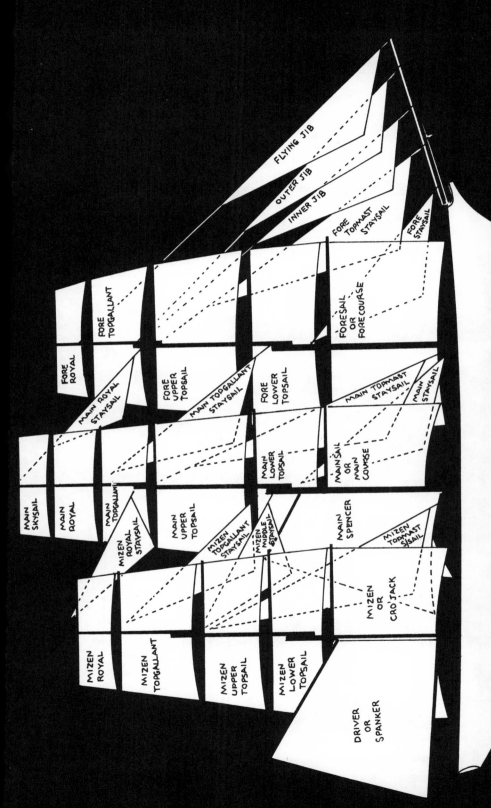

Full Rigged Ship

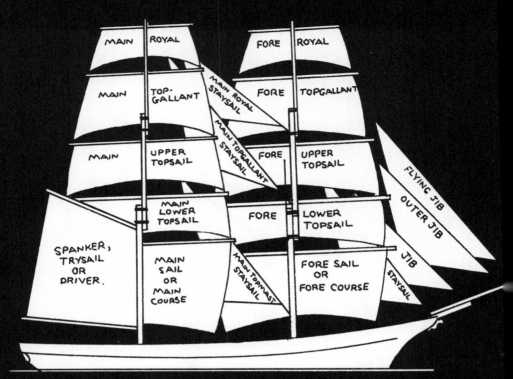

Brig

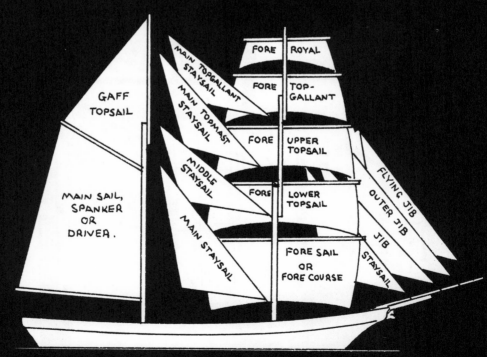

Brigantine

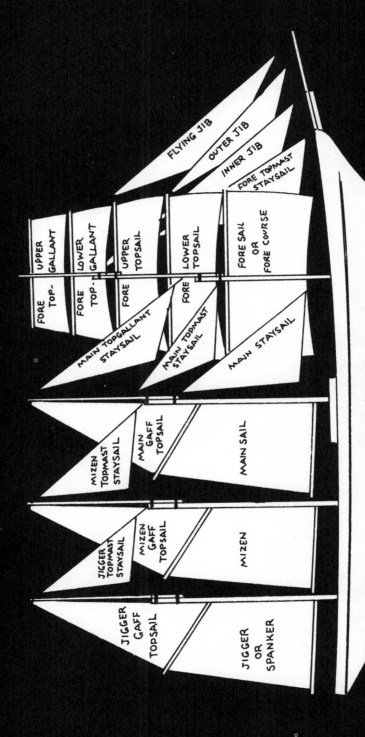

Barquentine

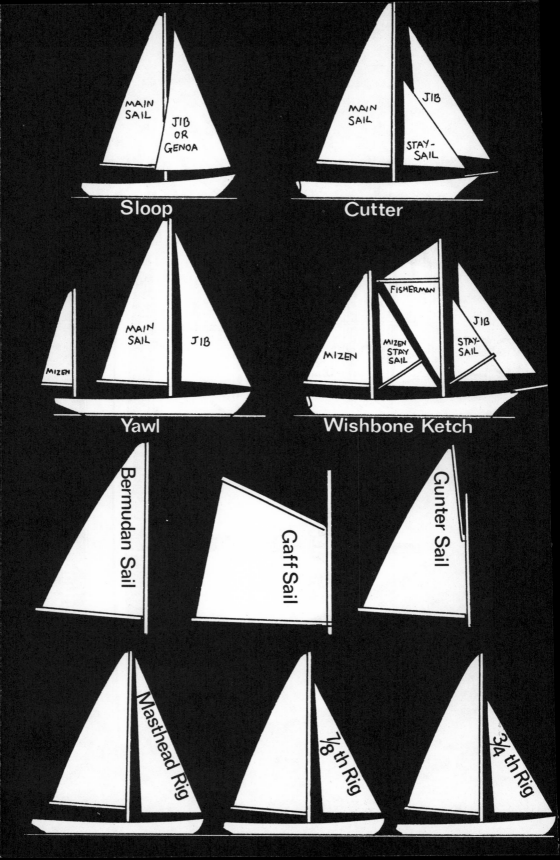

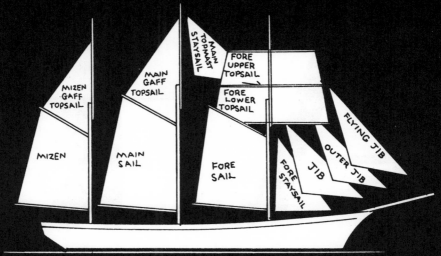

Three Masted Topsail Schooner

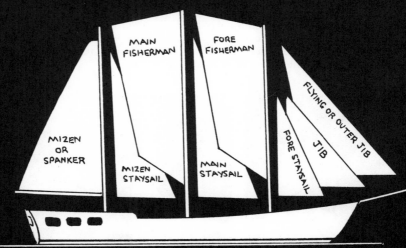

Three Masted Staysail Schooner

Ketch

Schooner

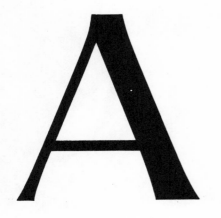

A. Code flag of the International Code of Signals with a single meaning, 'I have a diver down; keep well clear at slow speed'. It is a white and blue flag as shown.

ABACK. Said of a sail when the wind bears on the foreside of it. Done purposely it is said to be 'brought' or 'laid aback' when the intention is to heave to. When done unintentionally it is said to be 'taken aback'. In either event the vessel tends to drive to leeward.

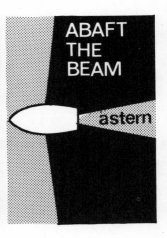

ABAFT. In the direction of the stern from whatever object is being referred to. For example, abaft the mast means towards the stern of the vessel from the mast.

ABAFT THE BEAM. Any object, when related to a vessel's position, is said to be 'abaft the beam' when bearing more than 90 degrees from dead ahead.

ABATE. When a wind reduces in speed.

ABEAM. When an object is at right angles to a vessel's fore and aft line.

ABOUT. Changing from one tack to another. Thus the terms 'put about' or 'going about'.

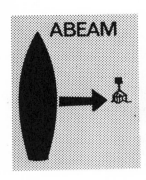

ABOX. Said of yards when those on one mast are braced in the opposite direction to those on the next mast. In this state a vessel loses way and can be held in a more or less stationary position. Commonly done when two ships 'talked' at sea.

'A' BRACKET. A self bracing strut for supporting the propellor. Commonly employed in twin screw installations where there is no keel extension to carry the load.

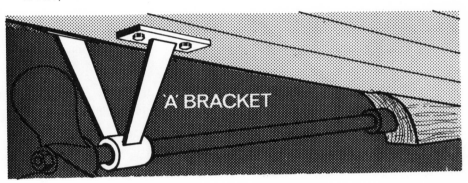

ABREAST. Said of two or more ships sailing parallel courses. Abeam of each other.

ACOCKBILL. The state of a yard when set to an angle other than 90 degrees to the mast. Done when being used as a derrick or to prevent outboard projection when berthing. Also said of an anchor hanging from the cathead by the cathead stopper only.

ACROSS THE TIDE. The state of a vessel during windward-tide conditions when the wind is strong enough to hold her beam on to the tidal flow.

ADJUSTABLE SKEG

ADMIRALTY SWEEP

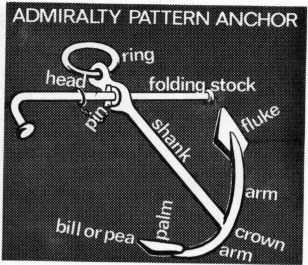

ADMIRALTY PATTERN ANCHOR

ring
head
folding stock
pin
shank
fluke
arm
bill or pea
palm
crown
arm

ADJUSTABLE SKEG. An external propellor shaft support with a moveable end which permits final adjustment to shaft angle.

ADMIRALTY CHARTS. Charts produced by the Hydrographic Department which is a division of the Ministry of Defence, Taunton, Somerset, England.

ADMIRALTY HITCH. See marline spike hitch.

ADMIRALTY PATTERN ANCHOR. Old type of anchor with folding stock. The shank and arms are fixed. A similar type with a fixed stock is known as the fisherman's anchor. Both types are ideal for general work but suffer from easy fouling because of the fluke that always projects from the ground.

ADMIRALTY SWEEP. Said of a small boat coming alongside when she approaches by way of a wide semi circle.

ADVANCE. Distance a vessel travels between the time the helm is put down and when she fully responds.

ADZE. A mattock-like tool used in the boatbuilding trade to shape large pieces of timber.

AFORE. In the direction of the bow from whatever object is being referred to. For example, afore the cockpit means towards the bow from the cockpit.

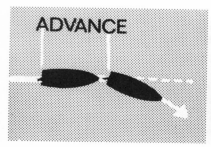

ADVANCE

ADZE

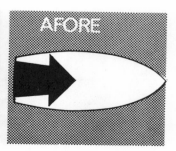

AFORE

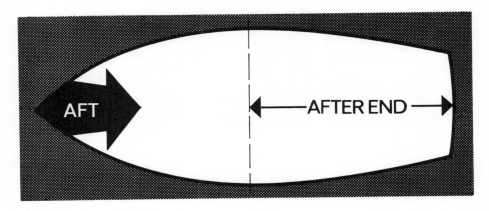

AFT. Towards, near or at the stern. Applied to wind it means wind blowing over the stern from 45 degrees to either side of it.

AFTER END. The stern half of a vessel.

AFTER LEECH. The vertical edge of a squaresail which is to leeward when sailing close hauled.

AFTER PEAK. The bulkhead area immediately forward of the transom forming a stowage area. In surveyed vessels this bulkhead must be water tight.

AFTER SWIM. The shaped underwater section of a hull giving a sweep-in of water to the propellor and rudder.

AFTERMOST. The object closest to the stern. Thus, in a two masted yacht, for example, the rear mast is the aftermost of the two. Also stated as 'aftmost'.

AHEAD. Direction of travel as opposed to astern. In the direction of the bow.

AHULL. Describes a vessel hove-to with all sails furled driven by the wind stern first or broadside on.

ALEE. Towards the opposite side to that on which the wind blows.

ALL ABACK. When all sails are aback.

ALL IN THE WIND. When sailing so close to windward that all sails shake.

13.

ALL STANDING. All sails set and working.

ALOFT. Anything above the highest deck is said to be aloft.

ALONGSIDE. Said of any vessel lying to a wharf or another ship.

ALOW. Below decks.

AMERICAN WHIPPING. A common whipping where the ends are brought up at the centre and reef knotted.

AMIDSHIPS. The area of a ship which is central both to the fore and aft line as well as the athwartships line. A helm order meaning to steer straight ahead.

AMPHIBIAN. Any craft capable of propelling itself on land or water. The Army Duck is a classic example.

ANCHOR. An implement which depends more on gripping power than deadweight to hold a ship in the one position. The types are varied but mostly stem from the Admiralty Pattern type, the parts of which are illustrated.

ANCHOR BELL. Placed forward, it is rung during fog as prescribed by law when a vessel is at anchor. Also rung to denote the number of shackles out when running out the anchor cable.

ANCHOR BUOY. An anchor position marking buoy. Consists of a buoyrope taken from the crown of the anchor to a small buoy. This also provides a method of tripping the anchor out of the ground should it foul.

ANCHOR CHAIN. See cable.

ANCHOR LIGHT. An all-round low powered white light hoisted at the forestay whilst at night-time anchorage. Vessels of over 150 feet must carry a similar light at the stern 15 ft lower than the bow light. Both must be visible from 2 miles.

ANCHOR POCKET. A shaped recess at the hawse pipe to permit the anchor to stow flush with the hull plating.

ANCHOR ROLLER. A fairlead over which the anchor cable leads. Usually fitted over the stem or to one side of a bowsprit.

ANCHOR WATCH. Vigilance maintained whilst a vessel is at anchor. In small boats this is only necessary when over doubtful holding ground or when a shift in the wind is possible. The best method of checking against dragging is to note two or more natural transit bearings such as two mountain peaks in line. If they open the vessel is dragging.

ANCHOR WELL. A small self draining cockpit set into the forward deck to accommodate the anchor with a flush fitting hatch over it.

ANEMOMETER. An instrument for measuring wind speed.

ANGULATED SAILS. A triangular sail with the upper cloths parallel to the leech and the lower cloths parallel to the foot. They meet at a girth band which runs perpendicular to the luff.

ANSWERING PENNANT. Used in conjunction with the International Code to acknowledge a signal. It is hoisted 'at the dip' when the signal is first seen and then 'close up' when understood.

ANTICYCLONE. An area of high barometric pressure around which the wind blows in a clockwise direction in the southern hemisphere.

ANTI FOULING. A specially prepared paint for coating the underwater area of a hull. By virtue of the poisons contained plus its wasting properties, weed and other marine life cannot readily attach themselves. A small boat should be anti fouled at least twice a year and ideally three times a year.

APEAK. Said of anchor cable when it is up and down and the bow of the vessel is directly above the anchor. In this state the anchor is ready to break out. Also describes yards when cockbilled in contrary directions.

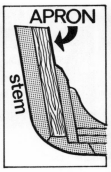

APOGEE. Point in moon's orbit which is farthest from the earth. Perigee is closest point.

APORT. Towards the port side. As an order means 'helm to port'.

APPARENT WIND. The actual direction and speed of a wind after the observer's position and motion is taken into consideration. For example; A motor boat driving 5 knots straight into a 20 knot wind experiences an apparent wind of 25 knots. A sailing boat beating to windward into a similar wind at 4 knots experiences an apparent wind of approximately 22 to 23 knots (because of its angle to the wind direction) which tends to head the yacht.

APPLE STERN. A rounded stern similar to the cruiser stern but with little if any centre-line visible.

APRON. The length of timber immediately behind the stem. The ends of the strakes land on the apron.

ARCHED. Old term for hogged. Describes a vessel that has sagged at each end from old age or continuous bad loading.

ARMING THE LEAD. Filling the hollow base of the sounding lead with tallow or grease so that particles of the bottom will be picked up and its nature ascertained.

ARMS. The extremities of a yard or boom.

ARSE. The lower or choke end of a common wood block.

ASLEEP. Describes a sail just filling as against flapping from lack of wind.

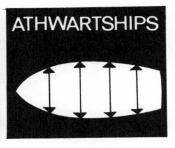

ASPECT RATIO. The relative lengths of the luff as against the foot of a sail. Thus a sail with a short foot and a long luff is known as a high aspect type.

ASTAY. Said of the anchor cable when its line tends to follow that of the fore stay.

ASTERN. Anything lying directly behind the vessel is said to be astern. (*See* Abaft the Beam).

AT THE DIP. Position of a flag when it is not hauled up close but is approximately two metres below the top of its travel. The answering pennant in this position indicates that the message has been received but not understood.

ATHWARTSHIPS. Any transverse line across a ship. From one side to the other.

ATRIP. An anchor that has just broken out of the ground. A sail hoisted and sheeted home but not yet trimmed.

AUSTRALIAN BOARD. The hinged platform extending from the transom of some motor cruisers to facilitate boarding, landing fish etc. The name is not commonly used in Australia but is often referred to as such by Americans.

AUTO PILOT. A machine that steers automatically. The controls are set when on the desired course.

AUXILIARY ENGINE. Any engine which is not the prime source of power. Thus the engine in a yacht is an auxiliary because the sails are the prime power source.

AVAST. An order meaning to stop, hold fast.

AWASH. Said of any item when the sea is just washing over it.

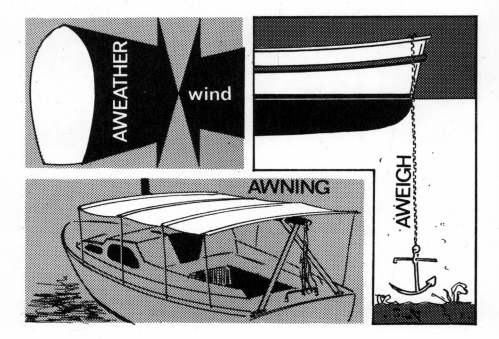

A'WEATHER. To windward.

AWEIGH. When the anchor is off the ground.

AWNING. A temporary canvas shelter from sun or rain.

AWNING LANYARDS. The small lengths of rope used to lash the awning down to the handrails or suchlike.

AWNING ROPES. Any rope that actually supports the awning. These are rare with the modern battened awning on small boats where mostly booms or poles are used for support.

AZIMUTH CIRCLE. An instrument which fits over a compass. It consists of a rotating arm which acts as a sighting bar and is fitted with a prism so that a compass reading can be taken whilst sighting an object. *See* Pelorus.

Photographs opposite. Top: *Incorporated into this pulpit are two large anchor rollers, one on each side of the bowsprit. Not only do the man-sized rollers ease the pain of weighing anchor but their outboard position holds the anchors away from the hull where they do least damage coming aboard.* Centre: *Breakwaters are traditionally made of stone although modern practise is to use formed cubes of concrete. This one guards the entrance to a creek.* Bottom: *The term 'boat' applies to any vessel too small to give accommodation for crew or cargo below decks. These sailing skiffs, the popular Manly Juniors, are boats in this context.*

Above: *This boom cap permits the boom to revolve when being turned by the roller reefing at the gooseneck end. From the bottom of the swivel plate the mainsheet is taken and from the top the topping lift is taken.* Below: *When a bowsprit is long enough to perform the duties of both the bowsprit and the jib boom it is called a 'spike bowsprit' as shown here. Note the Bobstay Purchase at the end of the sprit. This is to slacken or tighten the bobstay.*

The single block shown here is fabricated from stainless steel and plastic. Beneath it is a twist shackle and a hook. The rope through the block is Silver Rope, noted for its fibrous nature.

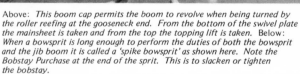

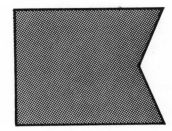

B. Second flag of the International Code of Signals meaning, 'I am taking in or discharging, or carrying dangerous goods!' It is a plain red flag.

BACK. Generally describes the act of reversing the motive force be it engine, sails or oars to drive the vessel astern. To back anchor is to move ahead over the anchor which is already down and drop another one ahead of it. In strict terminology, the two anchors are coupled together with a taught hawser or cable and the ship's cable is taken from a position between the two. A wind is said to back when it changes direction anti-clockwise.

BACKBONE. The fore and aft wire along the middle of an awning. Also loosely used to describe the keel of a vessel.

BACK SAILING. *See* Boxhauling.

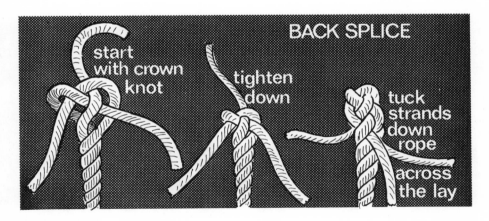

BACK SPLICE

start with crown knot

tighten down

tuck strands down rope across the lay

BACK SPLICE. Used to prevent the ends of a rope from unlaying when the rope is not intended to pass through a block. The strands are crowned then tucked back down the rope as shown.

BACKSPRING. A rope led aft from the forward cleat of a vessel to a point ashore. Used to prevent forward drifting or for heaving astern.

BACKSET. A current running in the opposite direction to the main body of water. Commonly occurs in bays along rivers.

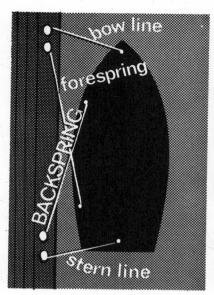

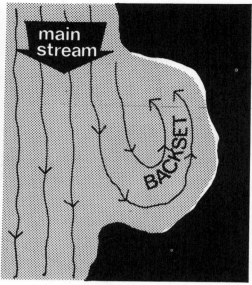

BACKSTAYS. Any stay employed to support the mast in a fore and aft line from the stern.

BACKWINDING. Caused by a foresail too tightly sheeted which directs the wind straight onto the leeward leading edge of the mainsail.

BAFFLE PLATES. Vertical and horizontal plates placed inside a tank to prevent its contents from surging.

BAGGYWRINKLE. (Also spelt Baggy Rinkle and Bag o' Wrinkle). An old-fashioned method of making up lengths of anti-chafe material to place on shrouds to prevent sail-chafe when squared away. It can still be used to great effect. It is made, as shown, by stretching two lengths of marlin close together between two suitable objects. 4-inch lengths of small diameter rope are cut and played out then fed onto the marlin and pushed hard up against each other. The marlin is seized at intervals to prevent the rope ends from falling loose. The lengths of marlin, with the rope ends in place, can be cut to suit various jobs. Most commonly they are lashed along the shrouds at intervals as stated.

BAGPIPE THE MIZZEN. To force the mizzen boom to weather until the sail is aback. It is part of the act of boxhauling as described later.

BALANCE LUG. This rig is similar in every way to the dipping lug (*See under* 'D' for diagram) with the addition of a boom along the foot.

BALANCED RUDDER. Where part of the rudder blade is forward of the stock. When turned, the leading edge moves away from the centre line of the vessel in the opposite direction to the trailing edge causing a balance of pressure on the forward area of the rudder.

BALDHEADED SCHOONER. A gaff rigged schooner with no provision for carrying gaff topsails.

BALDHEADER. A nickname for a square rigged vessel carrying no sail above the topgallants.

BALLAST. Any material carried either inside or outside a vessel to lower the centre of gravity and thus stabilise her. Originally called 'ballace'.

BALLAST TANKS. Compartments in large ships for fuel, water or other liquids that can be pumped from one tank to another to provide trim.

BALL HEAD TOILET. A recent design in marine toilets which utilises a soft 'bell' shaped lid that closes on the bowl forming an airtight seal. When the 'bell' is depressed, excreta is forced out through a valve.

BALLOON SAILS. Any extra sail carried for light weather work when the wind is abaft the beam.

BALSA SANDWICH. A fairly new technique in boat building which uses balsa as a core between inner and outer layers of fibreglass. The balsa must be laid in slabs with the grain on end to permit resin saturation.

BANDROL. (Also spelt Banderole). A small swallow-tailed flag flown at masthead as a wind direction indicator (See diagram under 'Tell Tale').

BANK. An area of shallow water in an otherwise deep section of the sea.

BAR. The silt bank which forms around the mouth of a river. Generally, there is always a channel which never dries at low tide but the surrounding banks tend to dry many feet in patches.

BAR CLEAT. A squat, 'T' shaped device which screws or bolts to a vertical or horizontal surface to which lines are made fast. There are many variations of the cleat which are described under their particular headings. Confusion often arises over the difference between a cleat and a bollard. As a general rule a cleat parallels the surface to which it is made fast and a bollard stands at right angles. There are, however, a few types that could be described either way as will be seen.

BARE POLES. Masts when no sail is set. More commonly used to emphasise severe wind conditions at sea, thus; 'she ran under bare poles', meaning no sail could safely be set.

BARGE. Any flat bottomed vessel whether self-propelled or dumb.

BARGE YACHT. A shallow draft, beamy sailing craft which is designed along barge principles. The 'Waterwitch' and the American Cat Boat designs are classic examples.

BARK. An alternative spelling to the word 'barque' which describes a three, four, or five masted sailing vessel fore and aft rigged on the after mast and square rigged on all others.

BARKENTINE. An alternative spelling to the word 'barquentine' which describes a three, four or five masted sailing vessel having square sails on the foremast only.

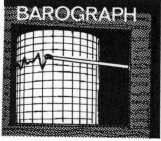

BAROGRAPH. An instrument which automatically charts barometric readings.

BAROMETER. An instrument for measuring atmospheric pressure.

BARREL BOLT. An ideal fitting for securing locker doors etc.

BATTEN CARVEL. Also called 'Ribband Carvel', describes a method of building wooden vessels where the planks run fore and aft and butt together flush on all edges and are roved down on an inside batten.

BATTEN DOWN. To securely cover a cargo hatch with one or more tarpaulins which are held around the edge of the hatch by battens and wedges as shown (cut-away view). This method is fast giving way to motor operated steel folding hatch doors. The term is generally used to mean the act of securing any vessel against bad weather.

BATTENS. Strips of flexible material (cane, fibreglass, nylon etc.) fitted into batten pockets along the leech of a sail to hold the leech out and maintain an even flow of wind across the sail. Most commonly used in mainsails.

BAY. Any indentation in the land that is wider than it is deep.

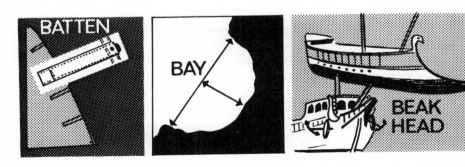

BEAK HEAD. Originally a metal covered projection from the bow of ancient ships designed to ram and pierce an enemy ship. Later, was a small deck built out over the bow of a ship.

BEAM. The widest part of a vessel. Any athwartships timber used to support the deck or so placed to withstand stresses on the vessel's side. This is also the old name for the shank of an anchor.

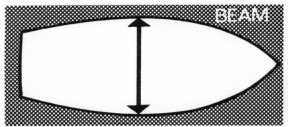

BEAM ENDS. Said of a vessel thrown down by wind and sea until her decks are almost vertical.

BEAM KNEE. Any gusset-like member that connects a beam to a frame. Originally a natural grown knee was used in timber construction. In modern materials such as fibreglass, ferro cement and steel, the identity of the knee is often lost being an integral part of the whole.

BEAM REACH. Sailing with the wind on the beam. *See also* Soldier's Wind.

BEAMY. Said of any vessel which tends towards extreme beam for her length. In small yachts, a beam of more than one third the overall length is considered beamy.

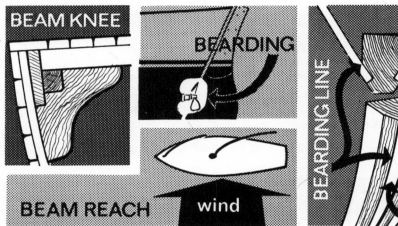

BEARDING. Term used in timber boatbuilding to describe the act of shaping wood to modify a curve. Typically, the rounded fore edge of a rudder.

BEARDING LINE. The intersection of the side of the stem and the surface of the rabbet into which the planks are fitted.

BEARERS. Any non-structural member in a vessel used to support another non-structural item. An engine bearer (or bed) is a typical example as are the transverse beams lying across the top of the keelson to support the floorboards.

BEARING. Direction in which an object lies from an observer. Navigationally it is stated as an angle between the observer and north (either true or magnetic but always magnetic in coastal navigation).

BEARINGS. Broad term to describe any fitting that supports a revolving shaft. The types are individually described through this book. *See* Cutlass Bearing, Thrust Bearing, Roller Bearing, Plummer Block.

BEATING. Sailing close to the wind (close hauled) on alternate tacks to reach a destination.

BEAUFORT WIND SCALE. A method of expressing wind speed by numbers. Each number refers to a range of speeds. Introduced in 1808 and revised in 1905 and again in 1926.

NUMBER	MILES PER HOUR	DEFINITION
0	0	Calm
1	1—3	Light airs
2	4—6	Light breeze
3	7—10	Gentle breeze
4	11—16	Moderate breeze
5	17—21	Fresh breeze
6	22—27	Strong breeze
7	28—33	Moderate gale
8	34—40	Fresh gale
9	41—47	Strong gale
10	48—55	Whole gale
11	56—63	Storm
12	64—71	Hurricane

Higher numbers can be used for worse conditions but are non-specific.

BECALMED. A sailing vessel is becalmed when there is no wind.

BECKET. A small loop in the end of a rope or wire, usually in a short length of line. 'Putting in a becket' refers to the act of lashing the wheel or tiller when the loop is placed over the spoke or tiller and the other end made fast to a cleat.

BECKET BEND. *See* Sheet Bend.

BECKET BLOCK. Any block with an eye beneath its tail to which the standing part of the tackle is taken.

BECKET ROWLOCK. A small loop of rope around the thole pin and an oar to contain the oar when rowing.

BECUEING. Describes a system of making the anchor fast to its cable in such a way that it will break out when extra force is applied. The cable is made fast to the crown then lightly lashed to the ring. In normal circumstances anchor will hold in usual way. If the anchor fouls, the extra force will break the lashing and the anchor is lifted by its crown.

BEE BLOCK. A small wooden block with a hole through which a line is rove. Usually on the side of spars.

BEETLE. Heavy wooden mallet used in caulking.

BEFORE. On the forward side of.

BEFORE THE BEAM. Said of any object observed to be forward of the beam but to either side of straight ahead.

BEFORE THE MAST. Said of a man who sailed on fully rigged ships and lived in the crew's quarters forward of the foremast (the forecastle).

BEFORE THE WIND. Sailing with the wind aft; 'running with the wind'.

BELAY. To make fast a rope around a cleat, bollard or bitt.

28.

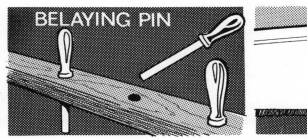

BELAYING PIN. A removable pin which sits in a pinrail and around which ropes are belayed.

BELFAST BOW. A bow that rakes forward from the waterline. Introduced by a Belfast shipbuilding company to provide greater space in the forecastle and to give reserve buoyancy when plunging into head seas.

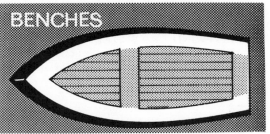

BELLY HALYARD. Gaff halyard leading through a block at the middle of the gaff. On small vessels this is usually part of the continuous length of the peak halyard as shown in the diagram. Strictly speaking the description should only be applied to a separate halyard doing this job.

BELOW. Under hatches. Below decks.

BELTING. A heavy rubbing strip of timber or steel placed at or near the waterline. The word is often erroneously used to describe any such rubbing strip regardless of where it is placed.

BENCHES. Any fore and aft seats in a boat. Seats across the beam are called thwarts.

BENCH-MARK. A mark cut into rock to indicate a datum level during survey work. British mark is a line and indicating arrow; American is a 3½ in. disc of copper.

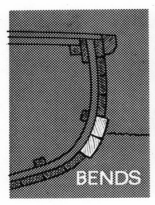

BENDS. Strong, extra thick strakes (planks) placed at and immediately above the waterline of large wooden ships. These give extra girder strength.

BEND SAIL. To attach a sail to its spar.

BENEAPED. A vessel that is stranded aground by neaping tides.

BENT TIMBERS. The ribs of a boat. So named because they are forced to conform to the shape as against being cut to shape.

BERMUDAN RIG. A general term indicating a masthead rig as against a gaff rig. The mainsail has only three sides and the mast is in one length.

BERTH. The space allotted to a vessel in harbour, be she alongside a wharf or at anchor. If at anchor it describes the full swinging area.

BETWEEN WIND AND WATER. That part of a boat's hull that is constantly covered and uncovered by wave action. This is the most vulnerable area for deterioration especially in steel vessels.

BIGHT. A loop in the end of a rope or any portion of a rope that hangs slack between two points.

BILGE. The underwater part of a ship's hull where the bottom plating meets the sides. On small boats, the area along the centre-line inside. Originally called 'bulge'.

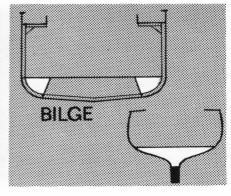

BILGED. Said of a vessel stove in anywhere along the bilge.

BILGE KEEL. Strengthening member placed fore and aft externally along the line of the bilge. It also protects when vessel takes the ground. Contemporarily, it means the relatively deep keel placed between the centre-line and the bilge. An identical keel is placed on the opposite side and together they provide reasonably shallow draught without sacrificing lateral resistance in small yachts. They can be associated with a centre keel but where there is no centre keel they are usually referred to as 'twin keels'.

BILGE KEELSON. A stringer laid fore and aft over the frames along the bilge.

BILL. The extreme end of the fluke of an anchor. Also called 'pea'. *See* Admiralty Pattern Anchor.

BILLBOARD. A ledge that supports the bill of the anchor when catted. *See* Catheads.

BINNACLE. Wood or metal stand in which the compass is housed.

BITTER END. The inboard end of a cable or rope which is made fast to a cleat or bitt. Named because the rope has been used 'to the bitter end' or because the inboard end suffers the least wear and is thus the 'better end'.

BITTS. Vertical timber or steel heads around which hawsers are taken for securing a vessel when berthing or towing. Also called Sampson Posts.

BITUMASTIC PAINT. A paint consisting largely of pitch (asphalt) which is a derivative of petroleum. It has no action on metals and remains elastic and waterproof. It can be used to advantage on rigging and general steelwork.

BLACK DOWN. To paint rigging from top to bottom in days when tar was used.

BLACKWALL HITCH. A quick self-jambing method of attaching a line to a hook as shown.

BLANKET. To sail close up-wind of another vessel and block her wind.

BLISTER. A compartment built on the outside of a ship's hull to minimise the effect of torpedo attack. Acrylic blisters, or domes, are sometimes used over hatchways of small ships, especially those used in cold climates where vision around the deck is required without venturing outside.

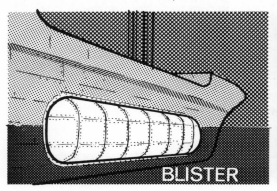

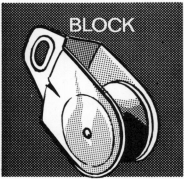

BLOCK. A pulley used to gain a mechanical advantage or to re-direct a line from one point to another. There are many types designated by the number of sheaves and their placement. The type shown on this page is a plain single sheave. For a full description of parts of the block turn to the heading 'Common Block'. For a description of how to rig blocks and rope into tackle turn to heading 'Tackle'.

BLOCK HANGER. A stainless steel fitting used for suspending a block from under a spar as shown.

BLUENOSE. A name applied to a Nova Scotian vessel or seaman. The vessels were mostly schooner rigged and were immediately identifiable by their distinct bow profile as shown.

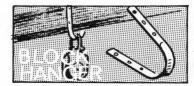

BLUE PETER. 'P' flag of the International Code of Signals.

BLUFF BOWED. Said of a vessel with broad, beefy entry. Typical of barge yachts. Full, bluff bows tend to incite a pitching motion.

BOARD. The distance between the point where a sailing vessel puts about and where she puts about again when beating to windward.

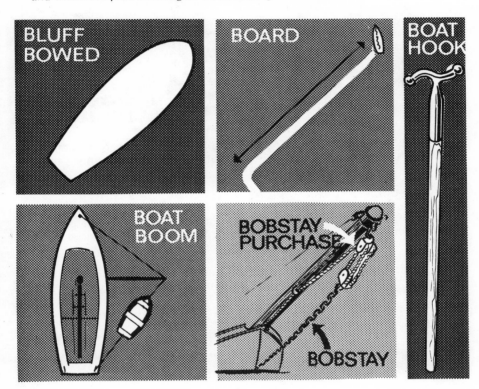

BOAT. In strict terminology, this is a small non-seagoing vessel propelled by oars only. Can be applied to any small vessel not intended for ocean work.

BOAT BOOM. A spar projecting from a vessel's side from which boats are secured in such a way that they ride away from the topsides. This is a particularly handy method for securing a yacht's dinghy when anchored in heavy windward-tide conditions.

BOAT HOOK. A long shaft with a hook at one end used for fending off, hooking onto, and picking up a mooring.

BOATSWAIN'S CHAIR. *See* Bosun's Chair.

BOBSTAY. Rope or chain between end of bowsprit and lower end of stem used to stay the bowsprit down against upward forces.

BOBSTAY PURCHASE. Consisting of blocks and tackle, a device for slackening and tightening the bobstay. Seldom used nowadays except where a long bowsprit is used and the bobstay tends to foul the anchor cable when at anchor.

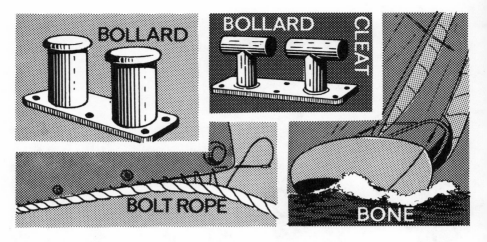

BOLLARD. Large vertical mooring post usually in pairs sharing same bolt-down base. This is different from the Bitt in that it is more an attachment than a part of the ship's structure.

BOLLARD CLEAT. A twin 'T'-shaped cleat.

BOLTROPE. The rope sewn onto the edges of a sail. Known by the part of the sail on which it is sewn thus; footrope, luffrope, etc. Superseded to a great extent nowadays by synthetic tape.

BONE. The foam that tends to pile up in front of the stem when under way. When excessive it is called 'having a bone in her teeth'.

BONNET. An extra sail used in light airs and set beneath the foot of a standing sail.

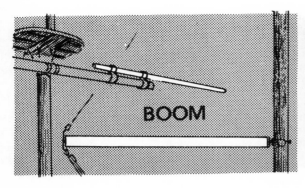

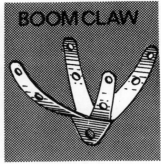

BOOM. Any spar used to extend the foot of a fore and aft sail. The name · 'Yard' is applied to the spars from which a square sail hangs although certain extra sails — such as studding sails — used on square riggers were set from booms.

BOOM CLAW. Similar in purpose to the Block Hanger but with four 'claws' to spread the load more evenly.

BOOM CRUTCH. A vertical, removable support for a boom when not in use.

BOOM GALLOWS. A boom support in the form of a lateral span on which one or more recesses for the boom are cut. Also doubles as an ideal awning fixing point.

BOOM HORSE. A metal collar with a wide 'ring' — or horse, which fits on the end of a boom to take the sheeting tackle. If the distinct horse is not included on this fitting it could more correctly be called a 'boom cap' or 'boom collar'.

BOOMKIN. Small spars projecting from a square rigger's side to sheet sails to and give them more spread.

BOOM SCISSORS. A collapsible support for a boom when not in use shaped like a pair of scissors.

BOOM VANG. A block and tackle system for holding down the central area of a main boom when squared away. This compensates for the inability of the usual sheeting system to prevent the boom from lifting.

BOOT TOP. The part of a ship's topsides between light and heavy loading. This area suffers the most from deterioration and is consequently coated with a different composition anti-fouling called 'boot topping'. In small vessels the Boot Top is for aesthetic purposes only.

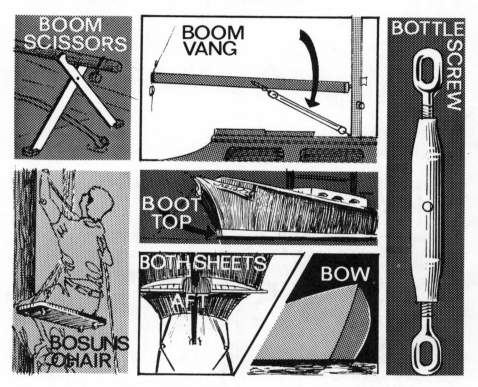

BOSUN. An abbreviation of the word boatswain. Originally spelt 'boson'. The officer in charge of ship's maintenance.

BOSUN'S CHAIR. A seat rigged swing-like in which a crewman sits to be hauled aloft. Originally made from a stave of a cask giving the seat natural shape.

BOTH SHEETS AFT. (1) A square-rigged ship running dead before the wind with both sheets of the square sails aft. (2) Said of a man swaggering along with both hands in his pockets.

BOTTLE SCREW. A specific type of rigging screw so named because the frame is fully enclosed forming a 'bottle'. *See* Rigging Screw.

BOW. The extreme forward end of the ship. The stem area. Also refers to the rounded part of a shackle.

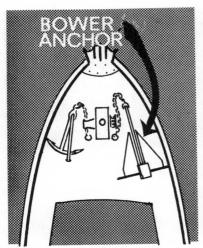

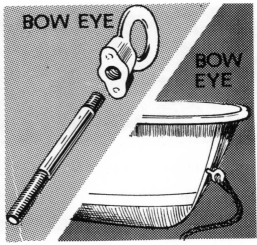

BOWER ANCHOR. The main anchor of the vessel. Normally carried on the starboard side and called the 'best bower'. Carried on the port side was a smaller anchor known as the 'small bower'.

BOW EYE. Pronounced as in *bow and arrow* — a type of eye bolt with the head removable from the actual bolt. The bolt is usually stainless steel and the head is chrome gunmetal. Ideally suited to any through-fastening eye bolt requirement but is not as strong. It does not foul ropes etc., so readily however.

BOW EYE. Pronounced as in *bow of a boat* — a general term used to describe any form of eye bolt through the stem of a dinghy.

BOW FAST. Said of a vessel moored or berthed by the bow.

BOW HANDLE. A small chromed fitting which can double as a cleat used to lift a small boat by the bow.

BOWLINE. As shown, a method of forming a loop or bight in the end of a rope in such a way that the knot cannot jamb during heavy use. Ideally suited to berthing lines but it should be emphasised that the knot cannot be undone whilst strain is on it.

BOW ROLLER. *See* Anchor Roller.

BOWSE. To pull down on a rope. To sweat down.

BOW SHACKLE. Pronounced as in *bow and arrow,* — a shackle shaped as shown.

BOWSPRIT. A spar projecting forward over the bow of a vessel. It is traditionally bedded down over the stem head and into the forward bitts. Its sole purpose is to spread the sail plan forward and outboard. Has tremendous sail balancing potential on small cruising boats.

BOWSPRIT CAP. A metal fitting over the outer end of the bowsprit from which forestay, bobstay and bowsprit shrouds are taken.

BOWSPRIT COLLARS. Bands around the bowsprit to take intermediate stays which help support the bowsprit.

BOWSPRIT SHROUDS. The rigging which runs from the bowsprit cap to each side of the vessel's bow and gives lateral support to the sprit.

BOX HAULING. A method of forcing a sailing vessel about when she threatens to refuse to go from one tack to another. The headsails are taken aback (clew to weather side) as soon as the wind starts to naturally back them and the mizzen is bagpiped immediately the turn is started.

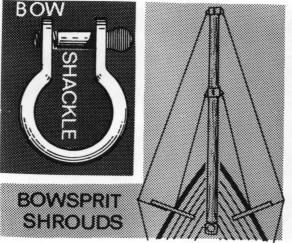

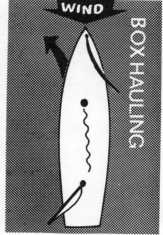

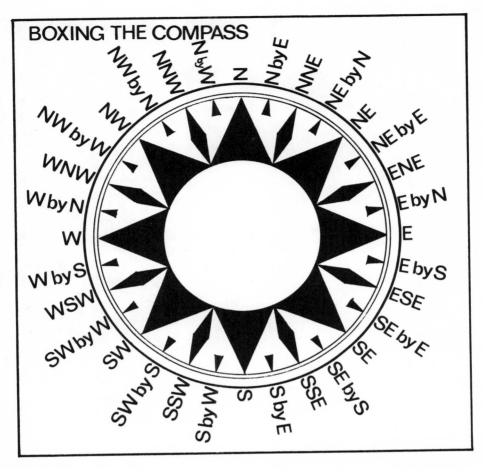

BOXING THE COMPASS

BOXING THE COMPASS. Reciting the 32 points of the compass. Each point is 11¼ degrees making it 4 points in 45 degrees, 8 points in 90 degrees and so on. Their names are stated in north, east, south and west segments.

BOX SECTION MAST. A hollow mast built like a box.

BRACE. The rope or tackle used to adjust a yard along the horizontal plane. They are led to a point on the mast immediately aft where they pass through a block thence down to the deck.

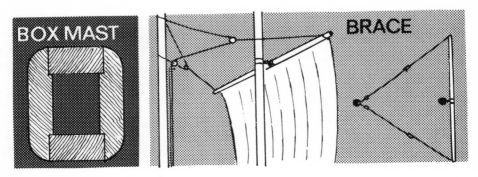

BOX MAST

BRACE

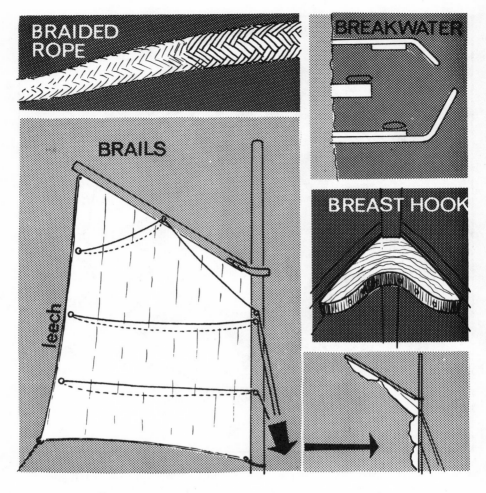

BRAIDED ROPE. A method of making up rope where three or more strands are interwoven in a diagonal pattern.

BRAILS. Ropes used for gathering in a boomless gaff sail towards the mast and gaff. A form of pre-furling. Lines run from the mast, around the leech through a cringle and back to the mast where they pass through blocks which direct them to the deck. This is similar to the method used for pre-furling square sails. *See* Bunt Lines *and* Clew Lines.

BREAK TACKS. Change from one tack to another.

BREAKING STRAIN. The point at which a rope, chain or wire will break when excessive loads are applied.

BREAKWATER. A man-made structure of rock etc., forming a wall into the sea that encloses a calm area.

BREASTHOOKS. Steel plates or timber knees placed horizontally between the fore ends of stringers to reinforce their marriage to the stem and apron.

BREECH. The lower aperture of a block. *See* Common Block.

BRIDGE. The wing extensions on each side of a wheelhouse on large ships from where the captain may see clearly fore and aft.

BRIDGE DECK. Any athwartships, main deck level, deck separating the cockpit from the main cabin.

BRIDGE EYE. A small fitting that performs the duties of an eye but the base is in two parts as shown.

BRIG. A two-masted vessel square rigged on both masts with a gaff mainsail on the after mast.

BRIGANTINE. Named because they were a ship of pirates (brigands); the brigantine has two masts, the fore mast being square rigged and the after mast fore and aft rigged.

BRIGHTWORK. Woodwork on a vessel which is varnished.

BROACH TO. Said of a vessel when she suddenly tries to round up into the wind whilst running free. This can occur by a particularly large wave or inattention on the part of the helmsman. Modern vessels with buoyant stern section and relatively slack fore sections are particularly notorious for trying to broach to.

BROAD ON THE BOW. Said of an object sighted more than 45 degrees from right ahead but before the beam.

BROAD REACH. Sailing free with the wind aft of the beam but not dead astern.

BULKHEAD. Any transverse or fore and aft partition in a ship. Not necessarily watertight but commonly so with full section bulkheads at the end of a vessel.

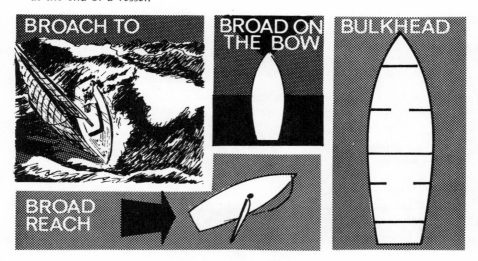

BUILT MAST. Any mast built of more than one piece of timber. Contemporarily, this could include any hollow section type, but in strict terms refers only to a solid mast where full length timber was unavailable.

BULL DOG GRIP. A U-shaped bolt over which fits a bridge that clamps down onto wire. Although very powerful, these should never be used permanently on rigging but are excellent stand-bys in case of rigging failure. The tail of the wire always lie against the U-bolt.

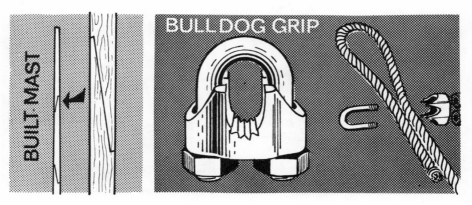

BULL ROPE. Name given to a rope led from the extreme forward end of a bowsprit down to a mooring, its purpose being to hold the mooring away from the topsides of the vessel.

BULL'S EYE. A shaped block of timber grooved around perimeter to take a strop with a hole to take a rope. Is in effect a sheave-less pulley. When this principle is used in tightening down standing rigging it is known as a dead-eye as described later.

BULL'S EYE FAIRLEAD. A similar fitting to a normal bull's eye but with a more pronounced base plate.

BULWARK. A planked in 'fence' around the edge of a deck to resist waves coming on deck and to protect crew etc.

BUMPKINS. Short fixed booms extending from each side of a square rigger's deckline near the bow to which the windward tack of a square sail is sheeted. Can also mean similar extension over stern to which mizzen is sheeted.

BUNK. A permanent place on which to sleep. Only referred to as such when a part of the actual fitments.

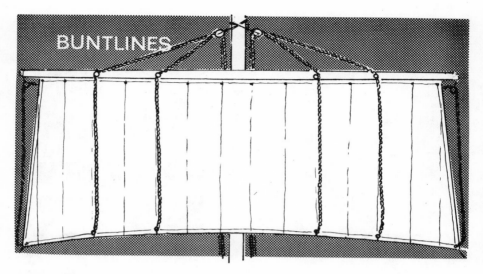

BUNTLINE. Used exclusively on a squaresail; a rope fastened to the foot and passing through a block at the yard, into the mast, thence down to the deck. Used to partially 'furl' a sail without going aloft. Similar in application to the clewlines.

BUOY. A floating object anchored to the seabed for use as a vessel's mooring or as a navigational marker.

BUOYANCY. The difference between the weight of the floating object and the upward pressure of the liquid in which it floats. Simply stated, it means the ability to float. *See* Centre of Buoyancy *for further information.*

BUOYANCY TANKS. Also called floatation tanks; air-tight compartments in a vessel aimed to give her floatation should the hull be damaged. In modern sail craft, these areas are commonly filled with expanding foam.

BUOYANCY VEST. A 'waistcoat-like' garment which gives positive buoyancy to the wearer.

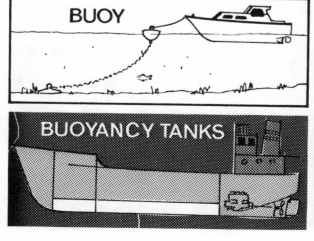

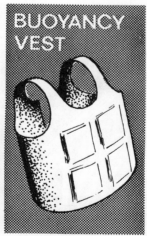

BURGEE. A swallow-tail flag.

BURTON. The name of a method of rigging tackle as shown.

BUTTERFLY BLOCK. A small snatch block with a long tail for general use around ship. Originally used for hauling in the deep sea lead.

BUTTERFLY VENTILATOR. A circular shaped ventilator with a hit-and-miss type operation usually fitted into bulkheads.

BUTT JOINT. Where two planks or plates meet flush and in close contact.

BUTTOCK. *See diagram.* Buttock Lines.

BUTTOCK LINES. Lines used in boat design and building to represent the fore-and-aft vertical sections equi-distant from the keel as shown.

BUTT STRAP. A short support plank or plate bridging across two planks where they butt together.

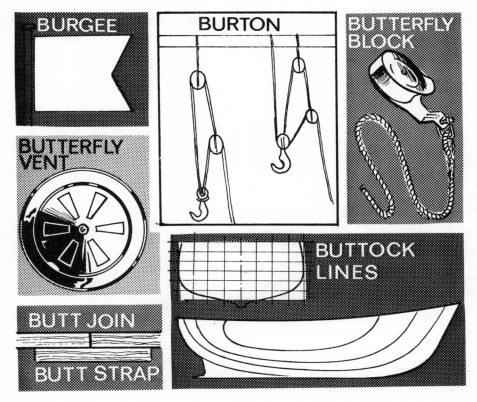

BY THE HEAD. Said of a vessel bow heavy caused either by poor design or clumsy stowage of gear.

BY THE STERN. Opposite to 'By the head'.

BY THE WIND. Said of a vessel sailing close-hauled but not as pinched up as she might be. Generally, when the sheets are just started she is said to be sailing 'By the wind'.

1. A dry dock is pumped clear of water behind sealed gates and the vessel within lands on chocks. Here the dock has been flooded to free the vessel within. 2. A typical older style of motor cruiser. Generally the term 'cruiser' is used to denote such a vessel. 3. This is a suction dredge. It works a pattern by winching itself along on anchors. 4. A sailing catamaran. 5. A modern version of the classic Cat-Boat. Strictly speaking it should not carry a headsail. 6. This unusual vessel is a catamaran-trawler. It is built of ferro-cement.

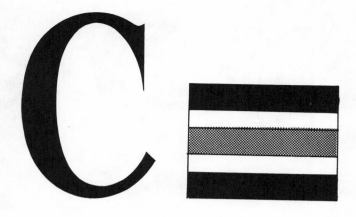

C. Flag of the International Code of Signals meaning 'Yes'. It is of horizontal bands; blue, white, red, white and blue.

CABIN. A small compartment aboard ship for officer, crew or passenger accommodation.

CABIN CRUISER. A motor boat with deck and deckhouse.

CABLE. A nautical unit of distance measuring 1/10th of a nautical mile (608 feet). 2. The chain or rope to which the anchor is made fast. Originally described the rope of more than 10 inches circumference used as anchor line in the days before chain. Ropes were then commonly 36 inches in circumference and were stowed in a huge circle aft of the fore-deck.

CABLE LAID. Four right-handed ropes made up into a left-handed rope.

CABLE SHACKLE. A shackle used for joining lengths of cable. Pin is flush with lug and is secured by a pin as shown.

CAISSON. The floating gate to a dry dock. Is floated in and out of position and is landed by filling with water.

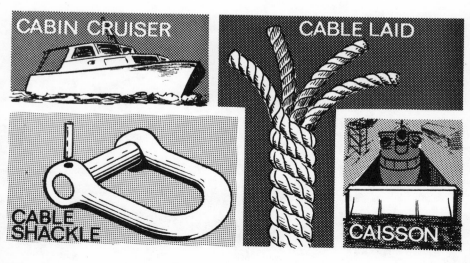

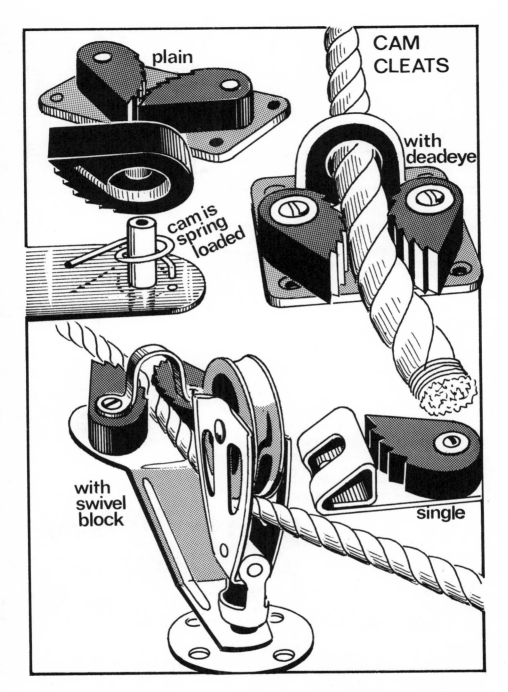

CAM CLEATS

plain

with deadeye

cam is spring loaded

with swivel block

single

CAM CLEAT. As illustrated above, a device which grips rope passing through it by the action of toothed cams that are spring loaded. Mostly used on sailing skiffs where loads are minimal and no permanency is expected. A handy type on larger craft for temporary holding of sheets and halyards. These are sometimes called 'jamb cleats' but this refers more correctly to non mechanical devices as shown under that heading.

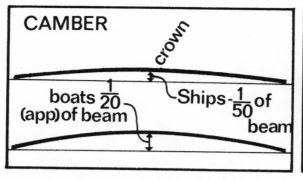

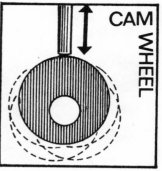

CAMBER. The curve of a deck. In large ships the standard camber is 1/50th of the vessel's beam.

CAM WHEEL. An eccentrically mounted wheel which imparts a reciprocating movement to anything bearing against it. Commonly used in valve mechanisms.

CANAL. An artificial waterway.

CAN BUOY. Believed to be a corruption of 'cone buoy', has cone shape underwater and flat top above water.

CANOE. A narrow beamed craft propelled by paddles.

CANOE STERN. Where the topsides terminate aft at the ship's centreline around fairly slack sections.

CANT. To tilt an object. Because this word was used to describe rolling over a whale whilst flensing, 'Cant Purchase' describes the tackles hung from the mainmast, hooked into the whale and used for rolling it over.

CANT RIBBON. A decorative moulding along a ship's side where it sweeps upward at the stern and bow.

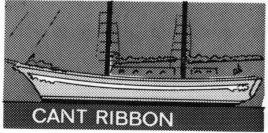

CAP. *See* Mast Cap.

CAPSTAN. A revolving barrel around which hawsers are taken when drawing a ship alongside etc. Can be power or hand operated. In its original form the barrel stood vertical with sockets around the top edge into which bars were fitted. Men walked these bars around, thus turning the capstan. The word 'capstan' can describe any winch drum.

CARDINAL POINTS. The four main points of the compass. North, East, South and West.

CAREEN. To haul a vessel over in the water so that the bottom may be scraped and painted. Can also describe tidal slipping.

CARLEY FLOAT. A life saving raft fabricated from floatation material.

CARLINS. Fore and aft members that support the ends of deck beams around a hatch or cabin aperture.

CARRICK BEND. A method of joining the ends of two ropes together as shown.

CARRY AWAY. Said of anything that parts company with the vessel such as a rope parting or a spar breaking.

CARRY HER WAY. When a vessel continues to move after the motive force has ceased is said to 'carry her way' until movement stops.

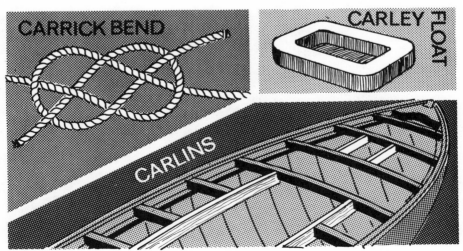

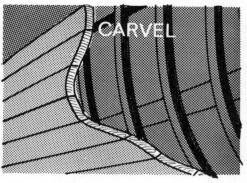

CARTOP DINGHY. A small boat, usually outboard powered but can be oars or sail only, carried upside down on the roof rack of a motor vehicle. Of necessity, it must be light enough for the average man to lift on and off and be sensibly proportioned to the vehicle on which it is carried.

CARVEL BUILT. A wooden vessel on which the planks run fore and aft and are laid against each other on edge to produce a smooth surface.

CARVING NOTE. Official note of authorization that vessel has been surveyed. It is carved into the main beam. In steel vessels it is usually shown by a weld run.

CASE. The name of the inner planking of a diagonally planked vessel. The outside planking is simply known as the 'skin'. *See* Cold Moulded.

CATAMARAN. Originally this could mean a craft which had more than one hull, regardless of the number. It is now used to designate any two-hulled craft.

CAT BOAT. This could describe any vessel that is cat rigged. It has been narrowed down to refer to a beamy, shallow draft centre-boarder used commercially in America last century. Its main features were the unstayed mast and the single gaff-headed mainsail. During light weather seasons the mast was sometimes moved aft and a headsail was set. It was nevertheless still referred to as a 'cat boat'. The type of boat is in no way related to a catamaran as is often thought.

CAT DAVIT. A davit used solely to lift the anchor once it clears the water.

CAT HEAD. A short beam projecting over the port or starboard bow — or both — from which a cat tackle is hung and is used to lift the anchor. Normal procedure was as follows; the anchor was weighed by its cable until the anchor cleared water. Because the anchor could not home into the hawse pipe (being before stockless types) a crewman climbed down, hooked the cat tackle into the anchor ring and the anchor was hauled up from the cat head. The crown was then hauled up to the billboard where it was lashed. If the ship were about to make a long passage, the cable would be released from the anchor ring and hauled up through the hawse pipe after which it was capped to prevent waves surging through it. A modified 'cat head' can be used by small boats to great advantage when using the Admiralty Pattern Anchor. As shown, the 'cat head' becomes a projecting anchor-cable fairlead. When weighed, the anchor is hauled up to this by its cable after which the crown is hoisted to the handrail or similar and lashed. It looks shippy and is very practical although it must be admitted that sheets and sails can easily foul on the anchor when stowed in this ready-to-use position.

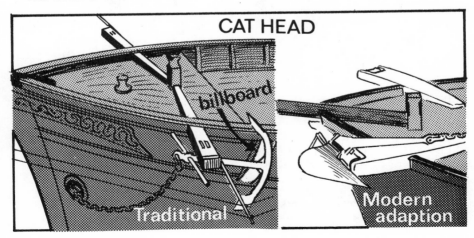

CAT HEAD

billboard

Traditional

Modern adaption

CATSPAW. Two loops formed from one bight of rope to take a hook. Also refers to a light puff of wind.

CATWALK. A long narrow walkway. The gangway over the decks of a tanker is a classic example.

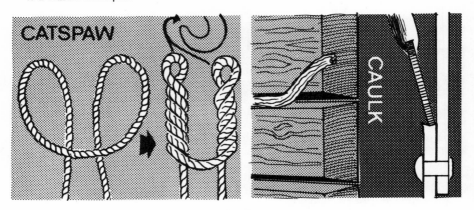

CAULK. To make a joint watertight by driving oakum or cotton between two planks in a timber boat or to expand the overlapping edges of steel plate by hammering the join as shown.

CAVITATION. The result of too much air around the propellor usually caused by the propellor being too close to the surface.

CAVIL. A short cleat close alongside the pinrail on square rigged ships.

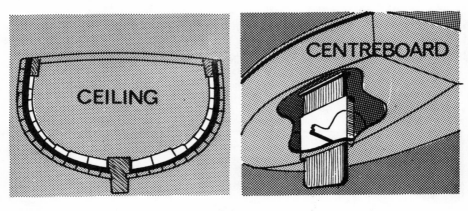

CEILING. The wooden covering over tank tops in the bottom of the hold. Commonly used to describe a timber lining around the entire inside of the hull as shown.

CELESTIAL NAVIGATION. The art of navigating by heavenly bodies when there are no landmarks available from which to take a bearing.

CENTREBOARD. A form of drop keel that lowers into the water from a case situated over or alongside the keel to increase lateral resistance when beating to windward. When the board operates in a similar style to a knife in a sheath it is called a dagger-board.

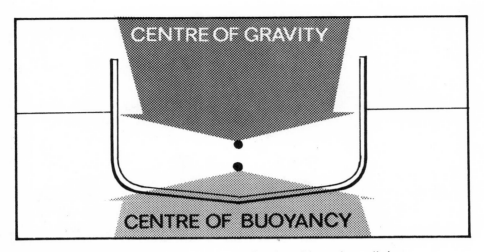

CENTRE OF BUOYANCY. The point in a floating object where all the moments of buoyancy are balanced by equal moments in the opposite direction. Thus, the centre of buoyancy in a perfect sphere would be in the exact geometric centre and would remain there regardless of movement. In a hull, where shape changes, the centre of buoyancy (abb. C.B.) moves. The fact that it moves in relation to the centre of gravity is the basis for any formula related to hull stability. The accompanying illustration shows this in its basic form. A more comprehensive illustration accompanies the description of 'Metacentre'.

CENTRE OF GRAVITY. The point in any body where the moments of gravitational force are balanced by the buoyancy of the object. *See* Centre of Buoyancy.

CENTRECASE. The watertight casing in which the centreboard homes.

CENTRE OF EFFORT. The geometric centre of a sail or the whole sail plan. In practise the centre tends forward of the geometric centre owing to the shape and softness of a sail.

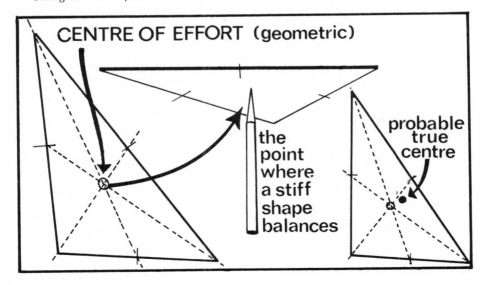

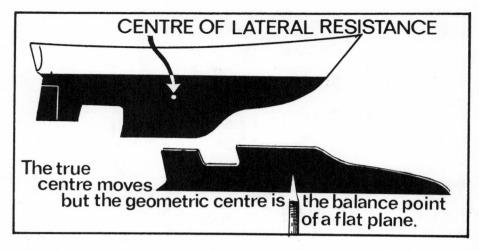

CENTRE OF LATERAL RESISTANCE

The true centre moves but the geometric centre is the balance point of a flat plane.

CENTRE OF LATERAL RESISTANCE. Assumed to be the geometric centre of the underwater profile. In fact the true position seldome lies here. It is the point from where a hull could be pushed sideways and both ends would move away at equal speed. The 'pivot' point.

CHAFING GEAR. Any material used to prevent a sail or rope wearing away when in contact with a solid object. Typical chafe areas are the mainsail or mizzen where they contact the shrouds when squared away. Baggywrinkle was an original form of chafing gear and is still in use but more commonly such material as sheepskin is used. For covering the ends of the rungs of a ladder going up the shrouds an effective protection is afforded by tennis balls, cut and lashed to these points as shown.

CHAIN CABLE. Anchor cable made from wrought iron.

CHAIN HOOK. *See* Devil's Claw.

CHAIN KNOT. A succession of loops in a rope, each loop being passed through the previous one.

CHAIN LOCKER. The area below decks — usually forward — where the anchor chain stows. Also called 'Cable Locker'.

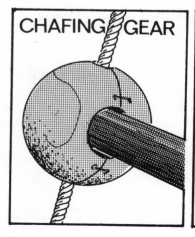

CHAFING GEAR

CHAIN KNOT

CHAIN LOCKER

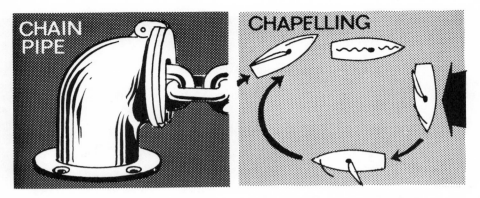

CHAIN PIPE. A general way to describe any pipe through which passes chain cable — usually the anchor chain.

CHAIN PLATES. *See* Shroud Plates.

CHAPELLING. The act of putting a close hauled vessel's head through the wind without intention and then having to wear right around until the course is resumed.

CHART. The 'map' used by boatmen. It shows depths, lighthouse positions, and characteristics and all information relevant to safe navigation. Depths are shown as the minimum at low water. This is known as 'chart datum'.

CHART ABBREVIATIONS. The standard abbreviations used on charts. These are available on a special chart.

CHART ROOM OR HOUSE. A special cabin set apart, but close to the helmsman, for the stowage and use of charts by the navigator. On small boats, where space is at a premium, charts are best stowed flat under the deckhead or a bunk and work carried out on the saloon table unless a separate table can be built of the dimensions of a chart fully opened (approximately 40 inches by 28 inches).

CHECK. To maintain control of a rope around a bitt or cleat whilst easing it out.

CHEEK BLOCK. A sheave fixed to one side of a spar etc., having half a shell.

CHEEKS. *See* Common Block.

CHEESE DOWN. Coiling a rope down flat on deck. Opposite way to the Flemish Coil. (*See* Flemish Coil).

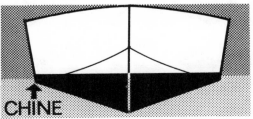

CHINE. The line where the sides and bottoms of a flat or 'V' bottomed craft meet. Originally called 'chime' after the rims formed by the projecting ends of the staves of a cask.

CHINSE. To fill a seam or crack with oakum or cotton.

CHIPPY. Knickname given to ship's carpenter. Now commonly applied to any boatbuilder or carpenter.

CHISEL SCRAPER. A long handled, resharpenable scraper used where barnacle infestation is extreme.

CHOCK. Any timber block used to rest various items such as the anchor.

CHOCK A BLOCK. Describes a purchase when the two blocks are as close together as possible.

CLACK VALVE. A hinged valve that opens by suction or force and closes by gravity.

CLAMP. The planks fitted to the inside of a ship's frames on which the deck beams rest. This is also called a 'deck shelf' but is oten used to refer to a separate plank immediately under the deck shelf.

CLAP ON. To make more sail, thus 'clap on sail'. Can also refer to the assistance given to someone hauling on a rope.

CLAPOTIC WAVES. The wave caused by the sea hitting a cliff face or similarly steep coastline, bouncing back and colliding with the incoming seas. These can be extremely dangerous and will rise to excessive heights.

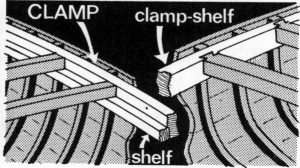

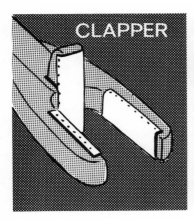

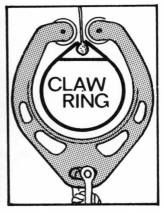

CLAPPER. 1. The tongue of a bell. 2. A chafing piece in the jaws of a gaff.

CLASS BOATS. Boats built from the same design so as to fall within the same
rules. This has become increasingly popular, eliminating, as it does, the
need to handicap individual craft.

CLAW OFF. Beating to windward off a lee shore.

CLAW RING. A horseshoe shaped metal ring that fits loosely around a boom.
Used with roller reefing from which to take a boom vang.

CLEAR VIEW SCREEN. A power driven circular inset in a window which
spins at high speed throwing off rain or spume by centrifugal action.

CLEAT. A wooden or metal fitting with two horns around which rope is made
fast. There are many varieties of the cleat which are dealt with under their
various headings throughout this book.

CLENCH. Securing a rivet or nail by placing a roove (or rove) over the inside
end then burring down over it.

CLENCH BUILT. *See* Clinker Built.

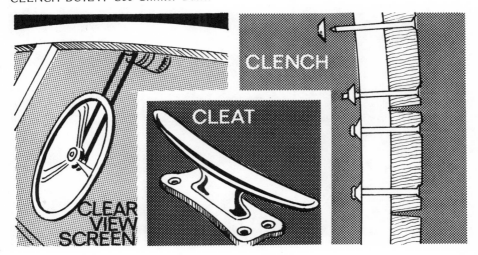

CLEW. The lower, after end of a sail. A square rigged sail has two clews, when one is to windward of the other they are known as the windward and leeward clews.

CLEW COUPLING. A fitting used to connect a sheet to the clew of a headsail consisting of two 'U' bolts which screw together.

CLEWLINE. Rope for hauling up the clew of an upper squaresail before furling. When used on a lower squaresail it is known as a 'Clew Garnet'. The principle is exactly the same. A rope from the deck passes through a block under the yard, (close to the mast) and makes fast at the clew. When hauled on the clew lifts to the yard and thus prepares the sail for furling.

CLEW UP. General term meaning to finish something. Comes from literal term meaning to raise clew of squaresail to yard and furl.

CLEVIS PIN. A small headed pin which is retained by the insertion of a split pin, or similar, through one end. Is used in shackles, rudder gudgeons, etc.

CLINCH. To join and fasten two overlapping planks using a nail which is passed through both planks and rooved on the inside as shown.

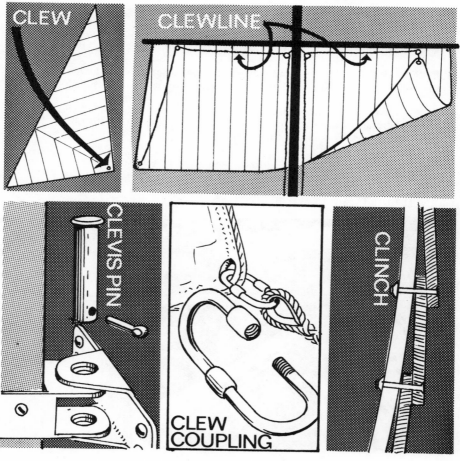

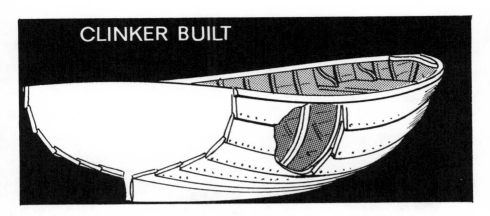

CLINKER BUILT

CLINKER-BUILT. A boat built with overlapping strakes (planks) which are clenched through. It is also called 'Clincher-Built'. This method gives a hull homogeneity and provides a way in which dinghies of minimum size could be constructed using natural materials. High speed craft gain a slight stabilising moment from the overlapping planks when constructed in this way.

CLINOMETER. An instrument used to measure the angle of heel of a vessel. It consists of a weighted pendulum which swings across a graduated dial.

CLIP HOOKS. Flat hooks that will only unite with their kind because of the bevelled, narrow-mouthed entrance. They are used wherever a quick, simple connecting device is required between two items, such as a guy onto a spinnaker pole. They are also called Sister Hooks.

CLIPPER. Name applied to fast sailing ships fine of line and with concave bow. The first built was the *Scottish Maid* in 1839. Because of their 'yacht' lines and light construction their carrying capacity was minimal and they required an enormous crew to handle them. They lost favour to the heavier, more cumbersome type of vessel towards the end of the 19th Century.

CLIPPER BOW. A bow which is concave in profile.

CLIPPER

CLIPPER BOW

CLOCK CALM. Completely calm weather.

CLOSE ABOARD. Said of anything that is close to the vessel.

CLOSE HAULED. Said of a vessel sailing with the wind forward of her beam. Generally refers to a situation where the vessel is sailing as close to the wind as possible (about 45 degrees from dead ahead) although this can more correctly be called 'close jammed'!

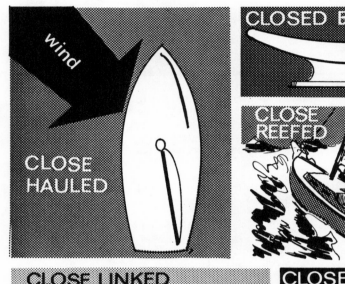

CLOSED BASE CLEAT. A common cleat with no hole or slot in the base through which a line can be taken.

CLOSE JAMMED. Sailing so close to the wind (close hauled) that any movement towards the wind puts the sails aback. Except for last minute attempts to clear a leeward object there is nothing to be gained by sailing so close winded. This condition is often referred to as being 'strapped in'.

CLOSE LINKED. Small chain which is not studded. Can also be referred to as 'short link' chain.

CLOSE REACH. Similar to close hauled in every way except that it usually infers that the vessel is not as close to the wind as it is possible to go.

CLOSE REEFED. Sails that have been reefed down as much as possible.

CLOSE WINDED. Said of any vessel able to go to windward with optimum efficiency.

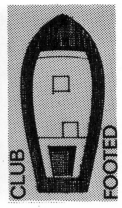

CLOVE HITCH. A useful, fast knot consisting of two half hitches as shown. This knot should not be used where excessive strain will be experienced as it readily binds and becomes impossible to free.

CLUB. The spar at the foot of any triangular sail. This generalisation could include a mainsail but it is never used thus. It always describes the spar used under a headsail and is given its full title of 'club boom'.

CLUB FOOTED. Said of a vessel with a wide forefoot (entry). Usually associated with the 'cod's head and mackeral tail' type design.

CLUB TOPSAIL. An oversize gaff topsail which requires that 'clubs' be used to extend both the mast and gaff as shown.

CLUMP BLOCK. A heavy duty block having a larger swallow than normal.

COACH BOLT. A generic term describing the common bolt. They are further described by the shape of the head. i.e., hexagonal head and cup head.

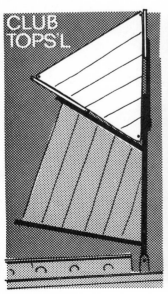

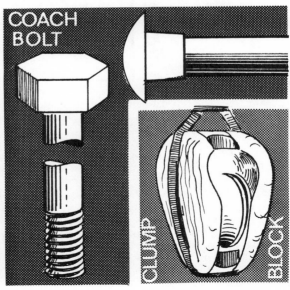

COACH HOUSE. Loosely describes any raised cabin on a hull but is most often used to name the highest part which is also called 'doghouse'.

COACH ROOF. The roof of the coach house. *See* Coach House *illustration.*

COACH SCREW. Also called 'lag bolt', a coarse threaded bolt intended to grip the timber without a nut. The receiving hole should be drilled as shown.

COACH WHIPPING. An ornamental or anti-chafe covering of small line or canvas over a larger rope, staunchion, etc. It is plaited down the host, as shown, after seizing the top. The bottom of the whipping is also seized.

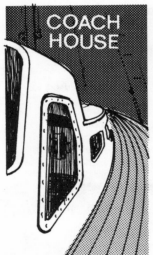
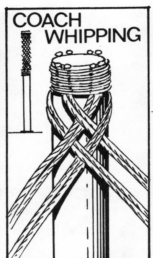

COAMING. The vertical 'fence' around a hatchway or cockpit. It prevents water slopping in and must be of a certain minimum height for survey standards.

COAST. (noun) That part of the land nearest the sea. (verb) To sail along close to the coast.

COASTGUARD. A body of men formed in England in 1817 and transferred to the Royal Navy, then H.M. Customs and now under Board of Trade, to suppress smuggling and watch for vessels in Distress. The coastguard in Australia is entirely voluntary and consists of enthusiasts who use their own boats and who man radio stations along the coast. Air Sea Rescue is a similar group.

COASTWISE. Along the coast.

COCKBILLING. *See* 'acockbill'.

COCKED HAT. The triangle on a chart formed by three position lines which, in theory, should all intersect at the one point. In fact they form a triangle and the vessel's position is within that triangle.

COCKPIT. A sunken area of a small boat, either amidships or aft, where the helmsman sits and from where all sheets are operated.

CODE PENDANT. Indicates that the International Code of Signals is being used. It is the 'answering' pennant.

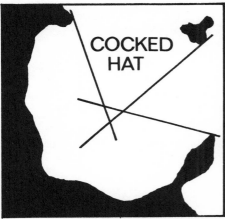

COD'S HEAD AND MACKERAL TAIL. Describes any vessel built with her maximum buoyancy foreward of amidships with consequent full bows and slack stern sections. This type runs off a sea very well with little or no broaching moment apparent but 'hobby horses' badly into a short sea and is generally a poor performer to windward.

COFFERDAM. The space between two bulkheads which isolates one area from another should one bulkhead leak. Also describes a temporary wall behind which rubble or cement is poured to form wharves, breakwaters, etc. Usually of 'U' section, interlocking steel sections.

COIR ROPE. A rope made from the fibrous outer covering of the coconut. Often referred to as 'grass rope'. This type has the least strength of all ropes and should not be trusted. It was ideal as a net float-rope before synthetics.

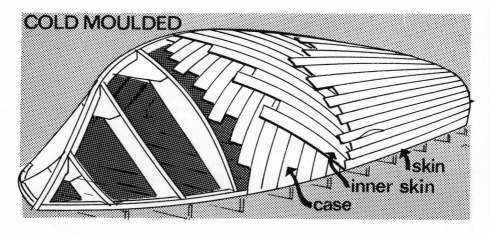

COLD MOULDED. A method of building light, strong hulls using two, three, or more, diagonal layers of either thin softwood or ply. The hull is built over a male mould which is later withdrawn and discarded and each skin is stapled and glued to each other.

COLLAPSIBLE BOAT. Any boat capable of being folded flat. Usually made of plywood or aluminium sides and bottoms joined with canvas or synthetic material.

COLLIER. A ship primarily built to carry coal.

COLLISION BULKHEAD. Specifically the first bulkhead back from the bow. Under survey requirements this should be free of any apertures and should be placed 0.05 percent of the vessel's waterline length back from the stem.

COMBERS. Large seas or breakers.

COMBINATION LIGHT. A navigation light combining red (port), white (masthead) and green (starboard) in the one housing for use on small boats only. This type does not comply with rules and regulations for large craft.

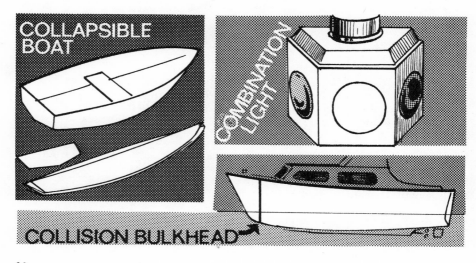

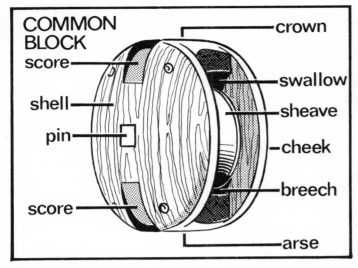

COMMON BLOCK

score

shell

pin

score

crown

swallow

sheave

cheek

breech

arse

COMMON BEND. The ordinary sheet-bend when not passed through a thimble.

COMMON BLOCK. A basic wooden block consisting of the parts shown in the illustration.

COMMON WHIPPING. A method of serving or binding the end of a rope using twine or marline as shown below.

COMPANIONWAY. The stairs or ladder leading to below decks.

COMPASS. An instrument used to ascertain direction. There are two types. One, the magnetic compass, is based on the attraction of the earth's poles. Two, the gyro compass, consists of an electrically driven gyroscope aligned with the earth's axis.

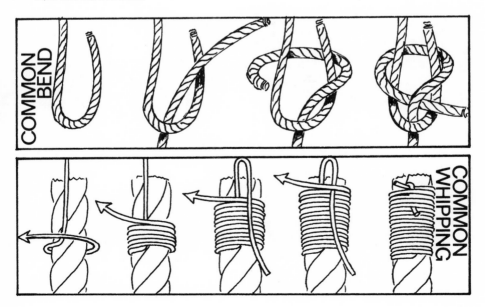

COMMON BEND

COMMON WHIPPING

COMPASS CARD. The circular card which is marked off in degrees (0 to 360) and is pivoted within the compass box.

COMPASS ERROR. The amount the compass is deflected by variation and deviation.

COMPASS ROSE. The compass 'card' printed on all charts. Were shown as magnetic rose, now shown as true rose with magnetic variation indicated.

COMPOSITE VESSEL. One built of steel frames and timber skin. Typically the strip planking method is used. The greatest disadvantage of this type lies in the fact that steel 'sweats' and the very pure moisture that results readily precipitates rot in the timber especially where extra areas of steel are incorporated to give added strength.

CONCRETE BOATS. A misnomer for ferro-cement construction. Concrete describes a conglomerate of sand, gravel and cement. In ferro-cement vessels the mixture is of sand and cement only with certain additives. *See* Ferro-Cement.

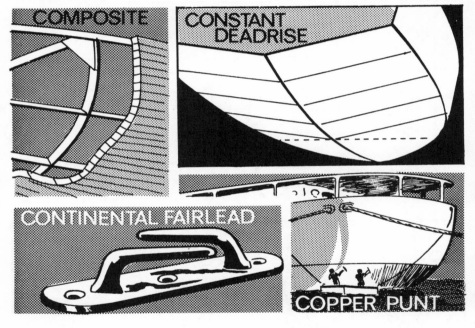

CONICAL BUOY. Buoy showing a conical shape above water. Can be used for any purpose navigationally, their purpose being displayed by their colours.

CONSTANT DEADRISE. Where the angle of the bottom plating of a vessel remains a constant angle to the horizontal plane from amidships aft. *See* Deadrise.

CONTINENTAL FAIRLEAD. A fairlead where the horns are angled in such a way that they permit easy entry of the rope but also effectively trap it. Also called the 'Skene Chock' named after its designer.

COPPER PUNT. A light raft used by large ships to support a crew in port whilst they paint between the waterline and the top of the anti-fouling.

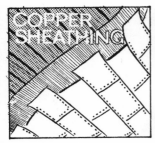
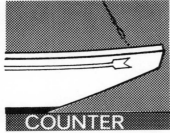

COPPER SHEATHING. Thin copper plates tacked to the bottom of a timber vessel which prevent fouling by exfoliating in sea water. Although still used extensively around keels, it has lost favour as an over-all covering in favour of modern anti-foulings, some of which contain copper dust as their main ingredient.

CORK GRANULES. Also called chippings, these are used to insulate bulkheads and also make an excellent deck surface. Ideally they should be distributed onto a latex-based glue after the surface has previously been brushed by diluted mixtures of glue and water.

COUNTER. The projecting stern of a yacht. Thus 'counter-stern'.

COUNTERSUNK SCREW. A wood fixing screw with a head so designed that it can be let into the surface of the job and thus be either flush or below it.

COVERING BOARD. The outside deck plank which covers the tops of the ribs. *See illustration opposite* Margin Plank.

COW HITCH. A simple slip knot as shown. Handy as a temporary method of gripping spars.

COWL VENTILATOR. The traditional type of ventilator. Mostly directional and readily adapts to the dorade box system. *See* Dorade Box.

COW TAILS. The unravelled ends of an unwhipped rope.

C.Q.R. ANCHOR. A trade name for the plough type mud anchor. Origin unknown but presumed to have been derived from the word 'secure'.

CRADLE. A frame of wood or steel used to transport or haul a vessel out of the water.

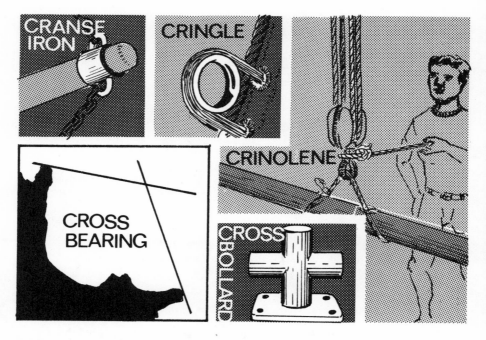

CRAFT. General description of any type of boat, large or small.

CRANSE IRON. A steel band at the outer end of the bowsprit to take the stays.

CRINGLE. Rope loop worked into the boltrope of a sail. May or may not have metal thimble.

CRINOLENES. Lines emanating from a purchase block and held in hand to steady a lifted weight.

CROSS BEARINGS. Two simultaneous bearings taken from different objects which are laid off on the chart to fix the ship's position.

CROSS BOLLARDS. A mooring bollard literally shaped like a cross.

CROSS TREES. Timbers fixed athwartships above the trestle trees to spread the shrouds. In modern use they are independent being used as shroud spreaders only.

CROWD ON. To carry maximum sail to facilitate a fast passage.

CROWN OF ANCHOR. *See* Admiralty Pattern Anchor *illustration.*

CROWN OF CAMBER. *See* Camber *illustration.*

CROWN KNOT. This is the first part of the back-splice. *See* Backsplice.

CROWS NEST. A platform mounted above the cross trees from where the lookout enjoys maximum safe vision.

CRUISER BOLLARD. A bollard (usually made of gunmetal) with its horns splayed out.

CRUISER STERN. A stern where the sides terminate at the centreline and the fullest part is at or below the waterline. Sometimes called a 'Bobtailed' Stern.

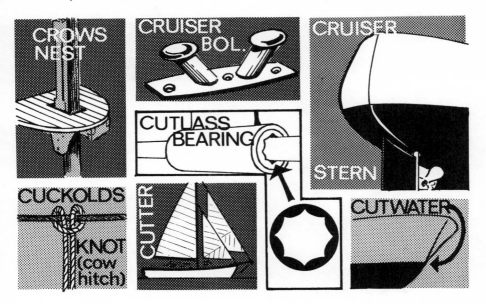

CRUTCH. *See* Boom Crutch.

CUCKOLD'S KNOT. Similar to a clove hitch but both ends exit in the same direction. Useful way of stowing ready-use lines on rails etc.

CURRENT. The horizontal movement of water. Always stated in the direction to which it is travelling. Thus a current moving towards the south is said to be 'setting' south and the rate at which it flows is called 'drift'.

CUTLASS BEARING. A synthetic bearing which inserts into a propellor shaft housing and is internally grooved to allow the free flow of water around the shaft to act as a lubricant.

CUTTER. A one masted vessel carrying two or more headsails, the outer sail being set from a bowsprit.

CUTTING. Tides are said to be 'cutting' when decreasing from springs to neaps.

CUTWATER. The forward edge of the stem.

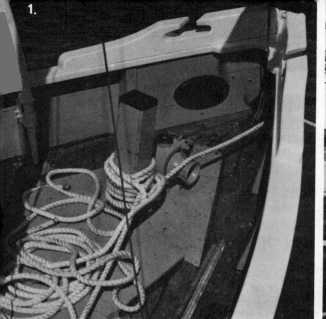

1.

2.

3.

1. A good example of a Bitt or Sampson Post. This was found on the famous Australian vessel Krait. 2. Whether of long overhang like the 30 square metre class bow in the foreground or of moderate overhang like the modern yacht behind, bows of this type are called 'Belfast Bows'. 3. A sprit overhanging the stern is known as a Bumpkin. This carries a permanent backstay clear of the mizzen boom.
4. A modern electric combination light is shown here. Red to port and green to starboard. 5. When a vessel is hauled down in the water or allowed to dry between tides she is being 'careened'. This type of careening is not the best treatment for a hull.
6. A Clear View Screen is a spinning disc of glass in the windscreen. 7. The boat depicted here is not a true dory. It is, nevertheless, referred to as a 'mackerel dory' in Queensland, Australia. 8. Built in the 1880s and still in commission, the gaff cutter Kelpie shows her superb counter stern.

4.

D

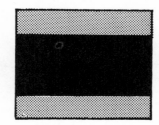

D. A flag of the International Code of Signals meaning 'Keep clear of me: I am manoeuvering with difficulty'. It is coloured yellow, blue, yellow, horizontal bands.

DAGGER BOARD. A type of centreboard which passes vertically through its case like a knife in its sheath. Used to increase lateral resistance on sailing boats large and small.

DAN BUOY. A spar with a balancing weight at one end and buoyancy material at its centre. Used as a marker. The high end is often fitted with a light which illuminates automatically and thus marks the position of a man overboard.

DANDY RIG. A single masted vessel with a small jigger mast right aft. Sometimes used to name a ketch or yawl.

DANFORTH. A trade name for a mud type anchor. The large flukes hold tenaciously giving an excellent weight-power ratio.

DAVIT. Projecting steel fitting from which is suspended dinghy, accommodation ladder, anchor, etc. *See* Cat Davit. Presents an ideal hoisting-stowing method for the dinghy of a yacht or cruiser, especially if placed over the stern.

DEADEYE. Rounded hardwood block, grooved around perimeter to take shroud-end and pierced with three holes to take lanyards. An old method of tightening rigging now usurped by rigging screws.

DEADLIGHT. The hinged shutter which clamps over a porthole.

DEAD RECKONING. The estimated position of the ship after taking into consideration speed, course steered and estimated leeway.

DEADRISE. The angle the bottom of a vessel forms with the horizontal plane. Always stated as the 'angle of deadrise' and it is taken from the midship section.

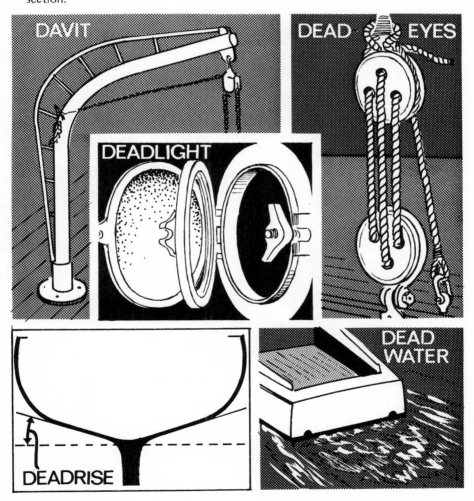

DEAD WATER. The eddy immediately astern of a vessel as she moves through the water. Pronounced on broad beamed sterns and especially if the transom enters the water.

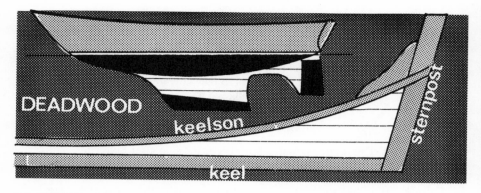

DEADWOOD. Non skeletal pieces of timber used to build up between keel and keelson at the stern (and sometimes the bow) of a timber vessel. On a modern fin-keeled yacht the deadwood is the 'dead' timber between hull and ballast.

DECK. Horizontal flooring, either partial or continuous, of a vessel.

DECK BEAM. Thwartship member which supports the deck and forms a firm non-collapsible 'bridge' between the sides of a hull.

DECK FILLER. *See* Filler (Deck).

DECK HEAD. The underside of the deck. The relative part of a house is the ceiling, a fact which causes considerable confusion. The ceiling of a boat is the 'lining' around the sides and bottom of a hull. *See* Ceiling.

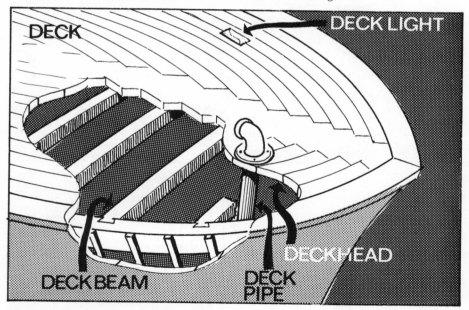

DECK LIGHT. Thick glass fitted into deck giving permanent natural light below. Can be in the form of a 'bull's eye' or prism. Both are designed to magnify the light.

DECK PIPE. The pipe through which the anchor chain passes from above decks to below decks. Also called a 'navel pipe'.

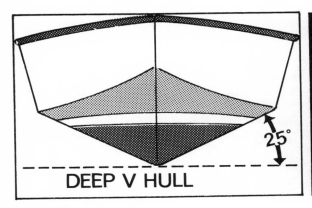

DEEP V HULL

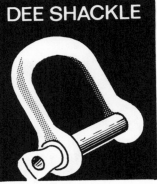

DEE SHACKLE

DECK SHELVES. *See* Shelf.

DEEP VEE HULL. A chine built boat with maximum deadrise. Usually about 25 degrees.

DEE SHACKLE. A shackle shaped as shown. This is the most common type.

DEPTH. The vertical distance from level of gunwhale to keel.

DERRICK. A boom used for hoisting and lowering heavy objects. The boom of any yacht can be used for this purpose.

DEVIATION. The compass error caused by the ship herself. Can be many causes but mostly from engine placement in small boats. Steel and ferro-cement boats suffer the most because of the quantity of steel and require more expensive compensating compasses than boats in other materials.

Deviation is the difference between true north and the direction in which the compass needle points because of shipboard influences. Ferro-cement and steel vessels are the worst offenders owing to the magnetic field within the steel.

Diaphragm Pump

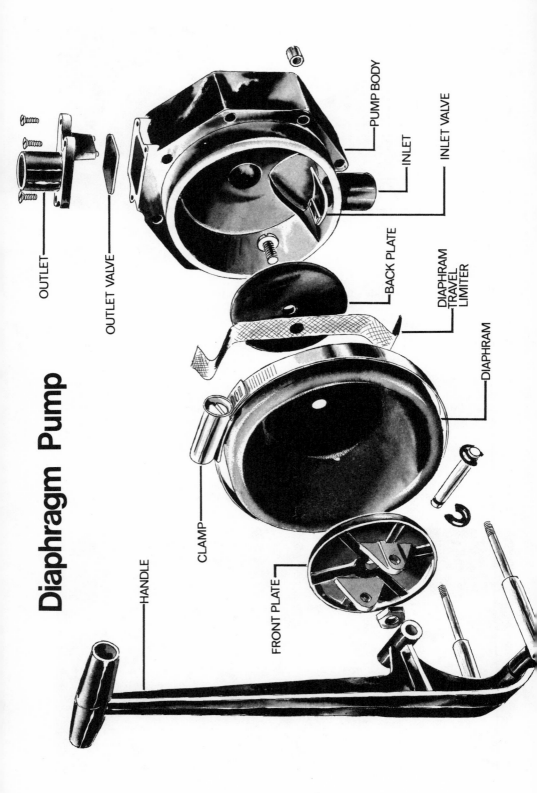

OUTLET

OUTLET VALVE

PUMP BODY

INLET

INLET VALVE

BACK PLATE

DIAPHRAM TRAVEL LIMITER

DIAPHRAM

CLAMP

HANDLE

FRONT PLATE

DEVIL'S CLAW. A temporary 'instant' method of stopping chain.

DIAGONAL PLANKING. Where one or more layers of a hull's skin is fixed diagonally to the fore and aft line. The old method, typically, would have two diagonal layers of timber over which a normal fore and aft layer is fastened. Between each layer red leaded canvas or tarred paper is fixed. The modern method is to glue each layer direct to the other skin (known as 'cold moulding' as described under that heading).

DIAMOND KNOT. Fancy bend in two ropes' ends made by interlacing them.

DIAPHRAGM PUMP. A self priming, maximum capacity pump which works by pushing a synthetic diaphragm into and out of the pump body. This type will pass large solids without fouling the valves although loss of suction can occur from excessive abuse. Ideal fresh water transfer, toilet flush and bilge pumps.

DIAMOND KNOT

DEVILS CLAW

DIPPING LUG

DIESEL ENGINE. An internal combustion engine which depends entirely on compression-for ignition. To be preferred aboard all boats although their extra weight-horsepower ratio denies them to certain small types.

DINGHY. Any small craft used as a tender for a yacht or motor cruiser. Also describes certain sailing skiffs.

DIPPING LUG. A 'tapered squaresail' with a spar along its head which has to be lowered partially so that the throat of the sail and the end of the spar, or yard, can be dipped around the mast when going about.

DIRTY WIND. The wind experienced immediately in the lee of a sail or object which is confused and non-directional and sometimes non-existent. It is called 'wind shadow'.

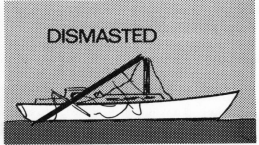

DISMASTED. Said of a yacht when her mast carries away.

DISPLACEMENT. The amount of water displaced by a floating body. The deadweight of the object is always the same as the weight of water it displaces. Thus a 10 tonne boat will displace 10 tonnes of water.

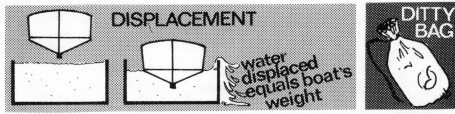

DITTY BAG. A canvas bag in which the seaman keeps his personal belongings.

DOCK. Is generally used to refer to any wharf or wall to which a vessel may be berthed — especially in America. Specifically it refers to an artifical enclosure for the berthing of a vessel.

DOCKING. Placing a ship in a dock.

DOCKING KEEL. Sometimes used to describe a bilge keel but only when such a keel is primarily incorporated into the design for the purpose of holding the vessel more or less upright when on the hard.

DODGER. Canvas fitted around parts of a boat to provide a windbreak for her crew. In small cruising yachts it is common to screen the cockpit as shown.

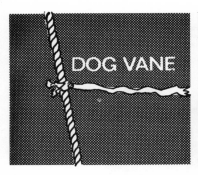

DOG VANE. A small length of material attached to the shrouds to indicate wind direction. Also called a 'tell-tale'.

DOG WATCH. The two two-hour watches between 1600 hours and 2000 hours (4pm and 8pm) to effect a change in pattern of the otherwise regular watch times of four hours.

DOGHOUSE. The raised part of the coachhouse or trunk cabin aft where an inside steering position can be placed and all round visibility can be enjoyed from below decks.

DOLLY. A heavy metal implement used as a portable 'anvil' when clenching nails or rooving.

DOLPHIN STRIKER. The vertical spar below the bowsprit to support the martingales of jib boom and flying jib boom. *See* Martingale *illustration.*

DORADE BOX. A method of providing perpetual ventilation in conjunction with (usually) a cowl ventilator. Air and water can flow in but only air can pass the internal bulkhead to flow below decks. Named after the yacht on which it was first used. *See next page.*

DORY. A flat bottomed double ender with flared topsides.

DOUBLE BLOCK. A pulley block with two sheaves on the same pin.

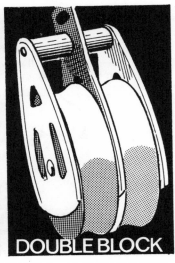

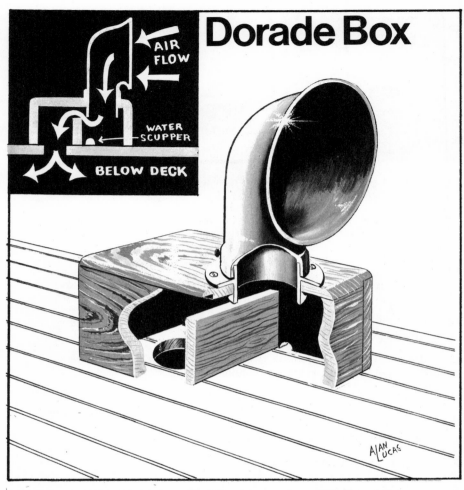

Dorade Box

AIR FLOW

WATER SCUPPER

BELOW DECK

ALAN LUCAS

DOUBLE CLEWED JIB. A four sided jib with two clews. Has the advantage of maximum area but defeats its object by being clumsy to bring about.

DOUBLE ENDER. Any boat where the topsides terminate at the stern at the ship's centreline. There are many forms including the canoe stern, cruiser stern and apple stern, all of which are described under their relative headings. Further information is given under the heading 'Heeled Waterlines'.

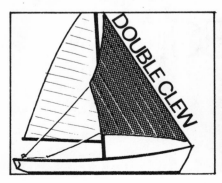

DOUBLE CLEW

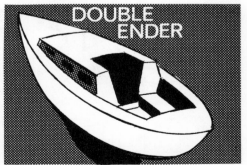

DOUBLE ENDER

DOUBLING. Any extra strengthening strip sewn into a sail or awning.

DOWNHAUL. A rope fastened to the top of a sail and led to the deck from where it can be pulled — or 'downhauled', to assist the sail to drop.

DRABBLER. A piece of canvas laced to the bonnet of a sail to increase the total area.

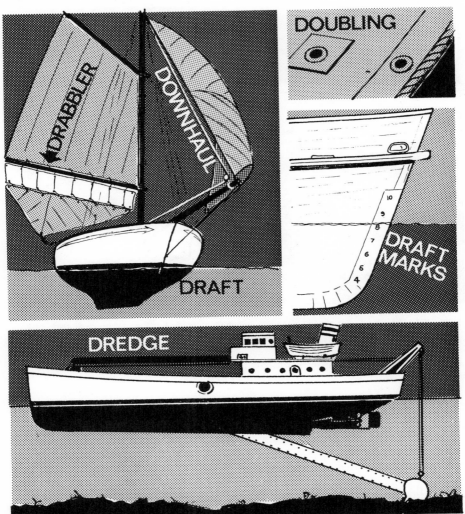

DRAFT. The depth of water at which a vessel floats. It is the amount she 'draws.' The word can also be spelt 'draught'.

DRAFT MARKS. Figures showing the depth of a vessel marked down the stern and stem.

DREDGE. A vessel exclusively used to excavate the sea bottom. There are various types, including the cutter dredge, bucket dredge and suction dredge. The correct word is 'dredger' but it is seldom used.

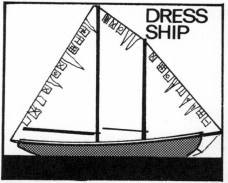

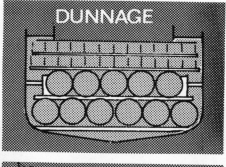

DRESS SHIP. To hoist a continuous line of flags from bow to stern over the masts. This is correctly called 'dressing ship overall'.

DRIFT ANCHOR. A drogue so designed that it resists passage through the water and thus, when fastened to a boat, holds that boat's bow into the wind. *See* Sea Anchor.

DROP KEEL. A general term to describe a retractable keel *See* Dagger Board.

DRY DOCK. An excavated dock with watertight doors into which a ship is placed. The doors are closed behind it and the water is pumped out leaving the ship dry and ready to work on.

DUMB BARGE. A work vessel with no sail or engine. It depends entirely on tugs to move it from place to place.

DUMB COMPASS. *See* Pelorus.

DUNNAGE. Battens and boards used to restrain cargo in a hold.

Photographs opposite. Top: *The main hatchway, through which most traffic passes, is called the 'gangway' or companionway. The lid is usually of a sliding type but this one hinges forward. A storm board fits into the vertical part of the gangway.* Bottom left: *This pretty stern belongs to an Atkins design 26 footer. It is called a 'canoe stern', both sides terminating at the centreline.* Bottom Right: *A view of a gangway from inside the vessel. The ladder could be called a gangway ladder or companionway ladder. The lighthouse is typical of automatic types along most coasts.*

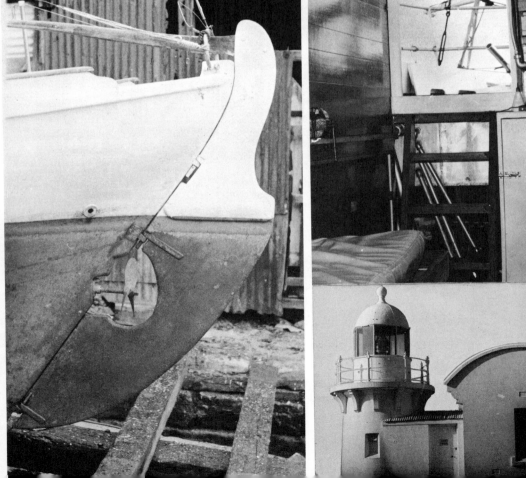

E. A flag of the International Code of Signals meaning 'I am altering my course to starboard'. It is coloured blue (above) and red (below) in two horizontal bands.

EARING. A length of line spliced into a cringle of sail or awning for fastening. Can also mean the outer top corners of a squaresail.

EBB TIDE. The receding tide.

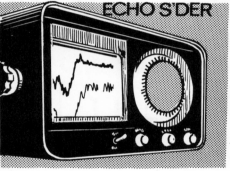

ECHO SOUNDER. An electronic instrument which emits a 'sound' from a transducer mounted on the bottom of a boat and measures the time interval until the echo returns. A graduated scale converts such information into feet and fathoms or metres. The inexpensive models have only a flashing light on a circular scale whilst the more expensive units also have a graph recorder.

EDDY. A current of water running contrary to the main, or host, stream.

EDGE NAILED. Describes a method of fastening. Specifically on strip planked vessels. *See* Strip Plank *illustration*.

EKEING. The ornamental carved work on after end of quarter gallery.

ELASTOMUFFLE. The trade name of an engine exhaust muffler made of synthetic rubber and depending greatly on its material to deaden noise. It also has a valve-like bulkhead within which alters and reduces sound waves.

ELBOW. Alternative name for knee.

ELECROLYSIS. The destructive action of salt water combined with dissimilar metals. The salt water acts as an electrolyte carrying an electric current from one type of metal to another. The less noble metal — such as zinc — becomes the anode whilst the most noble metal — such as bronze — becomes the cathode. The anode is always the one at which oxidising (wasting) occurs. Thus, to protect a vessel against electrolysis, an anode, in the form of a zinc pad, should be fastened externally to the bottom of the hull. This pad should be replaced when 10 percent has wasted for this is the most active portion. Pads should not be left on too long as old zinc can actually reverse the process of wasting so that an important fitting in the hull might deteriorate.

END FOR END. The reversal of rope, wire, chain or spars so the end taking the greatest load enjoys a respite and the non-working end takes the load. A halyard, for example, only works on the half from masthead to sail. End-for-ending extends the life twofold.

ENGINE. Can describe any form of motive power but by popular choice is used to describe any reciprocating power unit whilst the word 'motor' is used to describe fully rotary units such as turbines and electric motors.

ENSIGN. A National flag. Should be flown from the stern.

ENTRANCE OR ENTRY. The forepart of a hull.

EVEN KEEL. Said of a vessel when her keel is horizontal and her draught is the same fore and aft. Often used incorrectly to describe a boat which has no list.

EWBANK SPIKES. Also called 'dumps'. Thick, blunt nails used to fasten sacrificial chafing battens onto a timber hull. Especially used to 'dump on' the protective false keel over the coppered true keel.

EXPANSION CHAMBER. Name sometimes given to an exhaust muffler. The rapid expansion of gases is the main creater of noise. Thus, if the gases are allowed to expand within a chamber the noise is reduced by the time they are released into the atmosphere. It is possible to reduce engine noise to a whisper by using one or more oversize expansion chambers plus very long exhaust pipes. Space aboard small craft usually denies this luxury.

EXTRUDED MAST. A mast 'drawn' from a furnace in one 'extruded' length. Aluminium is the most popular metal in use although extruded steel masts have been used with success.

EYE. The loop of an eye splice.

EYEBOLT. A through-bolt with an eye at one end to which rigging etc., can be attached.

EYE AND EYE RIGGING SCREW. Where the two ends of the screw are both eyes.

EYE AND FORK RIGGING SCREW. Where one end is a fork, or jaw, and the other end is an eye.

EYELET. The brass grommets which are riveted through a mating hole in cloth. Consist of two parts as shown. Also describes a hole in material.

EYELET PUNCH. A tool consisting of punch and dolly used for riveting grommets to an eye.

EYE PLATE. A 'U' bolt sweated to a shaped plate which fits to the side of a mast to carry secondary rigging such as flag-hoist block, spinnaker pole etc.

EYE SPLICE. The forming of an eye in the end of a length of rope or wire rigging by tucking the strands back into itself. In ordinary three strand rope the ends are tucked as shown after which two to four more tucks are put in. Synthetic rope requires more tucks than natural fibre ropes.

EYE TERMINAL. A swage fitting which presses over the end of rigging and bolts by its eye to the rigging screw.

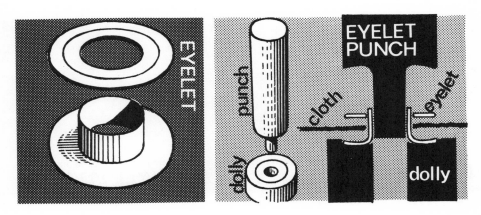

See over page for Eye Splice, Eye Terminal and Eye Plate *illustrations.*

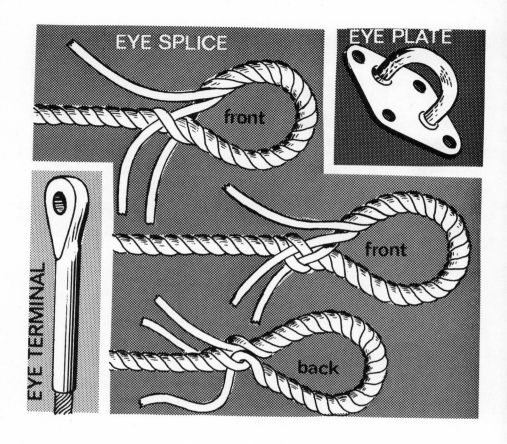

EYE SPLICE

EYE PLATE

EYE TERMINAL

front

front

back

A ferro-cement hull is constructed from layers of chicken or square mesh (or a combination of both) and steel rods. A typical lay-up would have eight layers of mesh with two layers of rods within the mesh. These rods should run longitudinally and transversely in that order from inside out.

This shows a good example of a flush deck yacht. Although a doghouse rises above it, the deck is essentially uncluttered being flush from stem to stern.

The frames shown here belong to a Sampson ferro-cement hull mould. The mesh and rod lay-up is draped over the frames and stringers, it is then tied off with staples which bind all the members tightly together then it is plastered with cement. When the cement has cured the whole shell is lifted off the wooden frames which are then either thrown away or used again for another hull.

90.

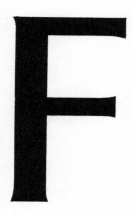

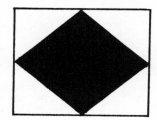

F. Flag of the International Code of Signals meaning, 'I am disabled, communicate with me'. A white flag with a red diamond in the centre.

FAG END. Unlaid end of rope.

FAIRING. The act of checking that a boat's lines are smooth and clean (fair) before the actual building. Final fairing is always done in the frame stage when frames can either be reduced or increased in size to eliminate any anomalies.

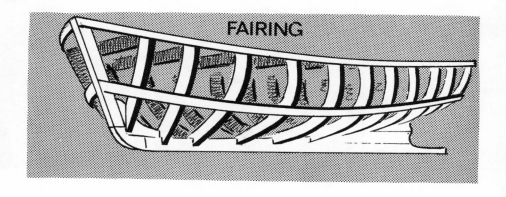

FAIRING

FAIRWAY. The navigable channel in or around a harbour.

FAIRWAY BUOY. The outermost buoy marking the beginning of the fairway (channel). Can be either a middle buoy or one of two port and starboard buoys. Called also the 'farewell buoy'.

FAIR WIND. A wind neither directly aft nor far forward of the beam. One which permits an easy sail not requiring a gybe or a work to windward.

FAKE. One circle of a coil of rope.

FALL. The hauling part of a purchase or tackle.

92.

FALL AWAY. Make leeway. To be driven sideways by current or wind. The arrows in the illustration show. 1. The wind or current. 2. The direction of drift. 3. The course steered and, 4. The probable true course over the ground.

FALL OFF. Movement to leeward of the vessel's head. Commonly after tacking until vessel picks up speed again.

FALSE KEEL. A sacrificial batten dumped onto the bottom of the true keel to provide protection.

FALSE STEM. An external piece fitted to the stem to produce a finer cutwater.

FALSE TACK. The act of going through the motions of intending to tack then resuming the same course. A trick in competitive racing.

FAST. Said of a vessel when alongside and 'made fast'. The word also applies to the hawsers with which she is fastened.

FATHOM. Six feet or 1.8 metres.

FAYING. Joining closely together. For example two plates welded together are 'fayed'.

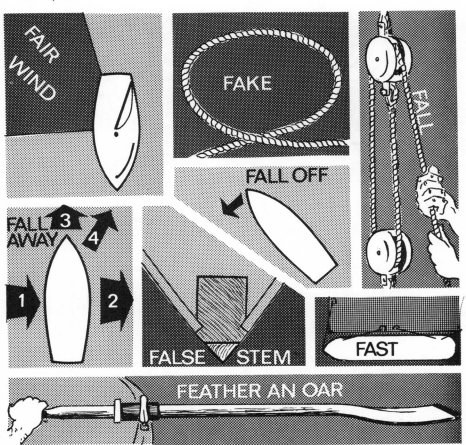

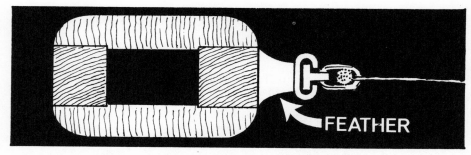

FEATHER

FEATHER. The batten along the back of a mast on which is fastened the sail track. It is not necessary but improves air flow and expediates bending on a mainsail.

FEATHER AN OAR. To turn the blade of an oar parallel to the surface of the water between each stroke.

FEATHERING PROPELLOR. A reversible-pitch propellor which, when the blades are neither propelling forwards or backwards, is 'feathered'. It is ideal where a gearbox cannot be fitted or adjustable pitch is required. Often used to describe the folding type as shown.

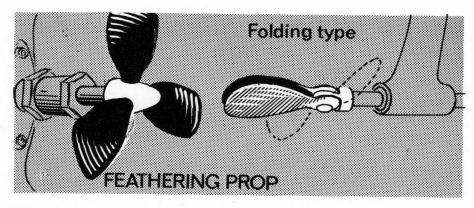

Folding type

FEATHERING PROP

FEED TANK. Any secondary tank in which liquid is held immediately prior to consumption. Typically, a small gravity tank above a diesel engine to which fuel is regularly lifted from the main tanks is a 'feed', or 'day' tank.

FELLOWS. The wooden pieces which make the rim of a steering wheel.

FENCE. The fore and aft vertical area between a fin keel and a rudder skeg. Incorporated into many modern hulls to impart strength and to add lateral resistance. Named after the 'fence' on aircraft which is the rising of the fuselage to the tail fin.

FENDER. A specially made buffer to hang between two vessels or vessel and wharf when lying alongside. Heavy fenders should be used as the modern lightweight types blow out of position and even up onto the deck during gusty conditions.

FEND OFF. To push or hold a boat clear so that she does not suffer topside damage.

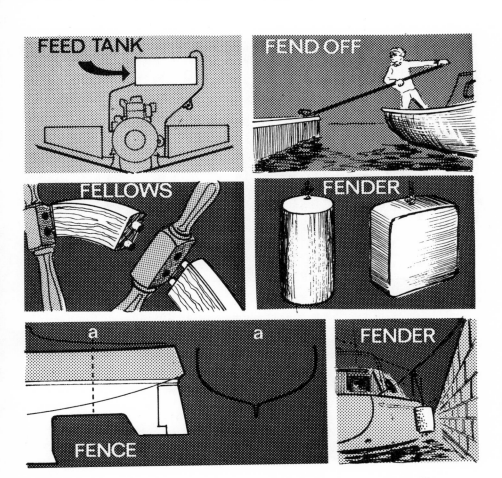

FEED TANK

FEND OFF

FELLOWS

FENDER

a   a

FENCE

FENDER

The 'ferro' in ferro-cement construction refers to the lay-up of mesh and steel rods. The mesh can be either chicken (diagonal woven) or square (weld) mesh or a combination of both. Survey requirements call for square mesh only. The rods (not shown) are sandwiched within the mesh.

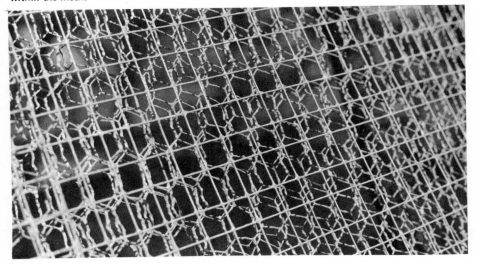

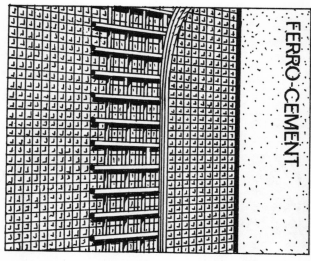
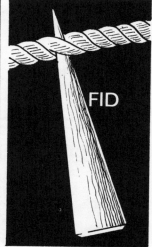

FERRO CEMENT. The combination of steel work and cement mix used to
    build boats of the same name. Essentially the hull consists of two to four
    layers of hexagonal or square mesh, one or more layers of steel rods then
    another two to four layers of mesh. This 'armature' is bound tightly
    together with wire ties, faired by panel beating, then cemented.

FERRY. Any vessel used to carry passengers across a harbour or river on a
    regular basis.

FETCH. The distance from point of origin to observer. Thus, a wind
    emanating from a disturbance fifty kilometers away has a '50 kilometer
    fetch'. In sailing it is to attain an objective. Thus, she 'fetched' the
    last buoy on the one tack. To fetch a pump is to prime it.

FIBREGLASS. Spun glass fibre made up into woven material or into
    chopped strand mats and rovings. Very popular in the construction of
    small craft where they are laminated and bonded by a thermosetting type
    plastic (polyesters being the most economical). This system is known as
    FRP (Fibre Reinforced Plastics) and GRP (Glass Reinforced Plastics).
    The strongest of the glass materials is the woven cloth. Chopped strand
    mat is ideal where maximum thickness—minimum cost is required.

FID. Large conical shaped length of wood used in splicing rope.

FIDDLE BLOCK. Also known as a 'sister block', this is a twin sheave block
    where the sheaves are in line instead of alongside each other. Has the
    advantage of not toppling.

FIDDLES. Detachable or permanent battens or rails which prevent the articles on a shelf from falling when the vessel heels at sea.

FIFE RAIL. Horizontal rail situated close to the mast in which fits a number of belaying pins. Halyards etc., are made fast to the pins.

FIGURE HEAD. The ornamental figure carved of timber and placed beneath the bowsprit.

FIGURE OF EIGHT KNOT. As shown, this is an ideal knot to place in the end of a rope to prevent it passing through a block or eye.

FILE SCRAPER. A scraper bent at one end to allow a pulling as well as a pushing moment when cleaning the bottom.

FILLER (DECK). A flush fitting plate and cap connected to tanks below by pipe.

FINE LINES. Said of any vessel possessing narrow beam with consequent knife-like entry.

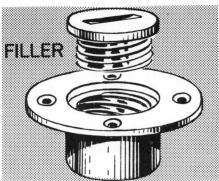

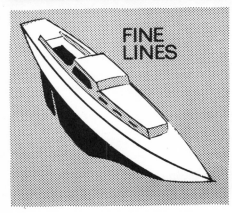

FISHERMANS BEND

FINE ON THE BOWS. Said of anything bearing up to 45 degrees from dead ahead.

FINE REACH. Sailing with the wind just forward of the beam.

FIRST MATE. The officer next in line to the captain. Is responsible for all facets of ship handling but especially the correct stowage of cargo.

FIRST WATCH. From 2000 hours (8 pm) to midnight.

FISHERMANS STAYSAIL

FISH. To strengthen a broken spar by lashing splints to it.

FISHERMAN'S ANCHOR. The oldest type of anchor. Simiiar to the Admiralty Pattern except that the stock is fixed. *See* Admiralty Pattern Anchor *illustration.*

FISHERMAN'S BEND. A bend for fastening a rope to an object as shown.

FISHERMAN'S KNOT. As shown, a simple method of joining two ropes together.

FISHERMAN'S STAYSAIL. Sometimes referred to simply as 'the fisherman', this is large topsail set above the main or mizzen staysail on schooners.

FITTING OUT. The act of rigging and furnishing a vessel.

FIX. The position of a vessel from two or more bearings taken simultaneously.

FIXED LIGHT. A navigational light, regardless of its colour which neither flashes nor occults.

FLAG-POLE SOCKET. A fitting made expressly to house the bottom end of a flag pole.

FLAKE. A single ring of rope. To flake a rope so that it will run free when required each flake is alongside the previous ring.

FLAKING A MAINSAIL. To furl a mainsail by laying it in bights on both sides of the boom.

FLARE. The outward sweep of a vessel's topsides. Usually only at the bow where additional reserve lift is achieved as well as a shedding action to oncoming waves.

FLASHING. A recurring light where its lighted period is shorter than the interval between appearances.

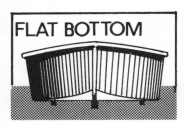 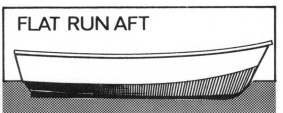

FLAT BOTTOMED. Said of a vessel possessing no deadrise whatsoever.

FLAT RUN AFT. A hull where the stern sections do not diminish greatly allowing buoyancy to be carried aft with consequent flat buttock lines.

FLATTIES. Flat bottomed dinghy. In Australia the term is most used in Queensland where it often describes any dinghy.

FLAT SEAM. Where two cloths overlap each other and are sewn down in that position.

FLAT SEIZING. This is used for binding two separate ropes together. It is essentially the same as a 'Round Seizing' which is fully described and illustrated under that heading.

FLEMISH COIL. Successive coils of rope laid down on the deck in such a way that each coil lies hard alongside the previous coil.

FLEMISH EYE. Made in the end of a rope. As shown, one strand is unlaid back, the two remaining strands are formed into an eye and the first strand is then relaid into the space from which it came in the opposite direction. The strands projecting down the rope are tapered, distributed evenly along the rope and served.

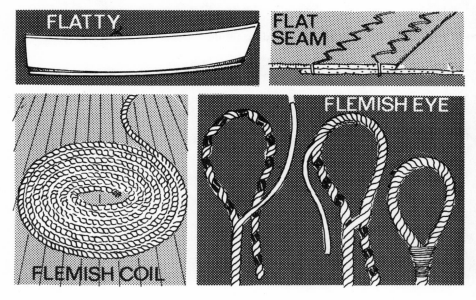

FLEMISH HORSES. Outer footropes on a yard to accommodate a crewman working right out.

FLEXIBLE WIRE ROPE. 6/19 around a fibre core is the most common flexible wire rope layup. It is so stated because there are 19 wires per strand and 6 strands per rope. Approximate breaking strain can be ascertained by doubling the square of the circumference in inches. The result is tons breaking strain.

FLINDERS BAR. Soft iron cylindrically shaped bars placed vertically on the fore and aft side of the compass to compensate vertical induced magnetism. Named after its inventor, Matthew Flinders.

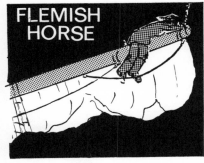

FLEMISH HORSE

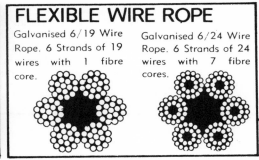

FLEXIBLE WIRE ROPE

Galvanised 6/19 Wire Rope. 6 Strands of 19 wires with 1 fibre core.

Galvanised 6/24 Wire Rope. 6 Strands of 24 wires with 7 fibre cores.

FLOATING DOCK. A dry dock which lowers itself into the water by the admittance of sea water into tanks then raises itself under a ship by pumping out the water.

FLOGGING. Describes a sail thrashing from side to side when unsheeted when the wind is ahead.

FLOODING. Said of a tide that is rising. The 'flood stream'.

FLOORBOARDS. The planking laid along the floors to provide a walking surface. Universally, called the 'sole'.

FLOATING DOCK

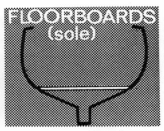

FLOORBOARDS (sole)

FLOORS. Transverse structural members lying beneath the floorboards which unite the hull's planking to the keelson and keel. *See illustration page 104.*

FLUKE. The triangular end of an anchor. *See* Admiralty Pattern Anchor *illustration.*

FLUSH DECK. A deck that carries unbroken along the sheer from bow to stern. *See illustration page 104.*

FLUSH HATCH. A hatch so constructed as to be flush with the deck yet not admit water below. Seldom entirely successful. *See illustration page 104.*

FLUSH RING. A fitting which enables a hatch to be lifted yet remains flush with the surface. *See illustration page 104.*

FLYING BRIDGE. A lightweight steering or observation area above the main deck.

FOLDING PROPELLER. *See* Feathering Propeller *illustration.* This type cannot be used astern.

FOLLOWING SEA. A sea that runs in the same direction as the course steered.

FOAM SANDWICH. A method of boat building in fibreglass similar to balsa-sandwich, except that synthetic foam is used in place of balsa for the core. There are many core types available made of polyurethane, polyvinyl chloride, etc. Boards of core material are lightly attached to a plug (male mould) then fibreglassed. When adequate skin thickness is built up the whole is separated from the mould, turned upright, and a second skin of fibreglass is laid onto the other side of the core which is the inside of the hull.

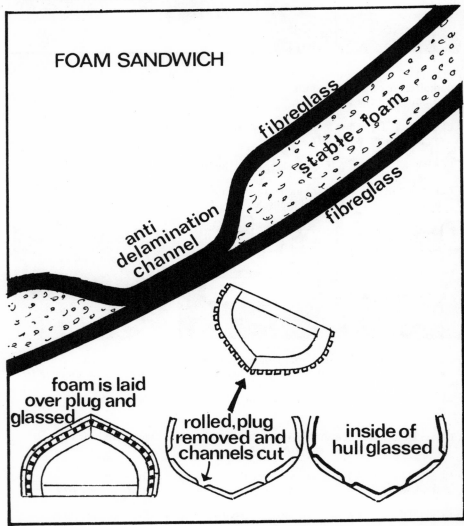

FOAM SANDWICH

fibreglass

stable foam

fibreglass

anti delamination channel

foam is laid over plug and glassed

rolled, plug removed and channels cut

inside of hull glassed

Photographs right. Top: *Foam sandwich or one-off pure fibreglass hulls are built over a plug or mould. As shown, the mould is built of timber frames over which battens are fixed.* Bottom: *'Gooseneck' is a general name given any fitting which unites a boom to a mast. Here we see a ratchet roller-reefing device incorporated into the gooseneck. It was built by Arvo Nokelainen, owner of the trimaran* Raili III.

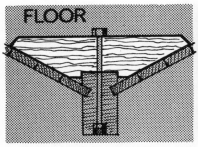

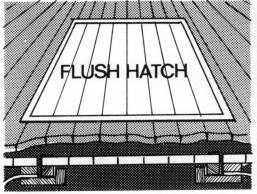

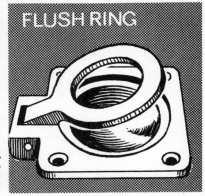

FOOT. Lower edge of a sail be it fore and aft or square. *See illustration opposite* Sail.

FOOTROPE. The rope along the foot of a sail 2. The rope which supports crewmen working out on the yards of a square rigger.

FORE AND AFT. Lying along the same direction as the length of the ship.

FORE AND AFT RIGGED. A sailing vessel carrying no squaresails.

FORE AND AFT SCHOONER. Schooner rigged vessel having no squaresails.

FORECASTLE. The first cabin aft of the chain locker. Named after a cabin which was originally above deck, forward.

FORE COURSE. The lowest sail on the foremast of a square rigged ship.

FOREFOOT. Where the keel joins the stem.

FOREMAST. The forward mast on any vessel having two or more masts.

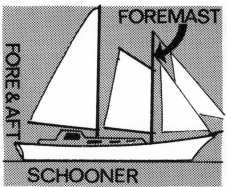

FORE & AFT

FOREMAST

SCHOONER

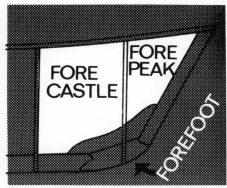

FORE
CASTLE

FORE
PEAK

FOREFOOT

FORECOURSE

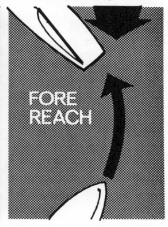

FORE
REACH

FORESAIL

FORESHORE

FORE PEAK. The space immediately aft of the stem and usually separated from the remainder of the vessel by a collision bulkhead. Chain and rope are normally stowed there.

FORE RAKE. The part of the bow overhanging a vertical line passing through the forefoot. *See* Belfast Bow.

FORE REACH. Making headway whilst going about.

FORESAIL. On square rigged vessels it is the same as the fore course. On two-masted schooners it is the 'main' sail between the masts (usually gaff). In one-masted vessels it can describe the jib.

FORESHORE. The area between low and high water marks.

FORESTAY. The wire rope running from the masthead to the end of the bowsprit or stemhead and preventing the mast from toppling aft.

FORK AND FORK RIGGING SCREW. One that has a fork at each end with which it is attached to chain plate and shroud.

FORK TERMINAL. A swage fitting for a shroud-end which attaches to the rigging screw by a fork.

FOUL. Said of the bottom of a hull when covered in weed and shell.

FOUL GROUND. Where the sea bottom is littered with rock outcrops, coral heads or wrecks and thus promises to foul the anchor.

FOUL HAWSE. Where a ship swings completely around on two anchors, the cables crossing each other and fouling.

FRAME. The transverse structure at each section giving form to a vessel being built. The frames are removed after completion and their function is replaced by ribs and bulkheads.

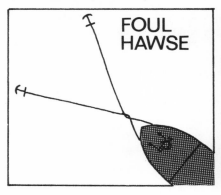
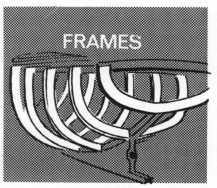

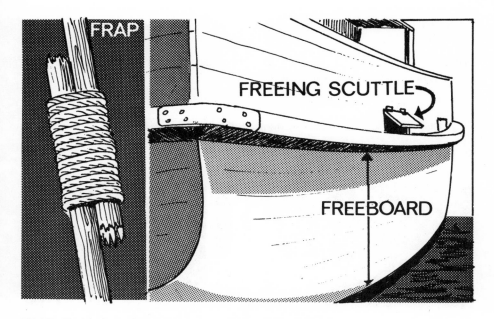

FRAP. To bind anything tight by passing a rope around it.

FREEBOARD. That part of the hull above waterline. Height usually measured to deck line at lowest point.

FREEING PORT. *See* Scuppers.

FREEING SCUTTLE. An opening in the bulwarks to permit water to escape off the deck which has a cover hinged in such a way that water is not permitted aboard again through the same opening.

FRENCH BOWLINE. Similar to bowline except that twin bights are formed as shown.

FRESH BREEZE. A wind of 17 to 21 knots. Force 5 on the Beaufort Scale.

FRIGATE BUILT. Applied to a vessel having a quarter deck and raised forecastle.

FULL AND BY. Sailing close hauled with sheets slightly eased and all sails filling.

FULL RIGGED. A square rigged vessel of three masts or more carrying all squaresails except for jibs and spanker.

FURLING. The gathering in of a sail and lashing it down.

FUTTOCK. The separate pieces forming a built rib of a boat.

FUTTOCK PLANK. The ceiling plank next to the keelson.

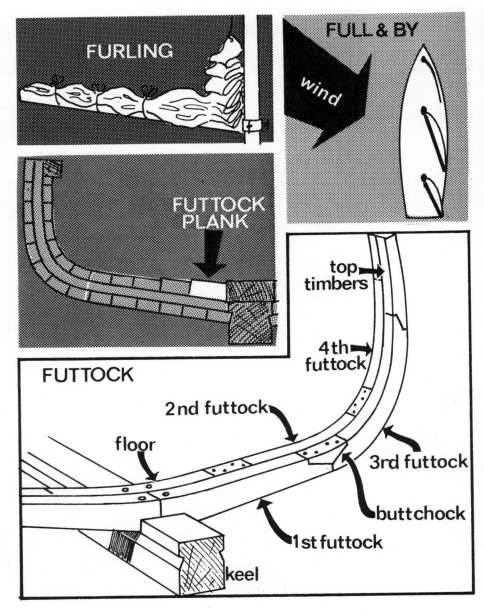

G

G. Flag of the International Code of Signals meaning 'I require a pilot'. When made by fishing vessels operating in close proximity it means, 'I am hauling nets'. It is coloured alternating yellow and blue vertical stripes.

GAFF. The spar to which the head of a gaff sail is bent. It fits to the mast by a simple jaw. *See Gaff illustrations on page* 116.

GAFF HEADED. A general way of referring to any vessel which has one or more gaff sails.

GAFF TOPSAIL. A triangular sail which sets immediately above the gaff and hoists to the topmast.

GALE. A strong wind. Under the Beaufort Wind Scale a gale is described as being a moderate gale (Force 7, 28 to 33 knots), a fresh gale (Force 8, 34 to 40 knots), a strong gale (Force 9, 41 to 47 knots) and a whole gale (Force 10, 48 to 55 knots).

GALLEON. An early Spanish vessel used in trade with South America. Distinctively high bow and stern.

GALLEY. 1. The captain's boat in the Royal Navy. 2. The cookhouse.

GALLEON

GALLEY BUILT. Name sometimes given to a flush decked sailing boat. *See* Flush Deck.

GALLOWS. Already described under the heading 'Boom Gallows', this word also refers to the structure from which a trawl net is slung from a trawler.

GAM. To exchange conversation with someone on another ship.

GAMMON IRON. The steel band clamping the bowsprit to the stem-head.

GANGPLANK. A portable 'bridge' between ship and wharf to allow safe access.

GANGWAY. Alternative name for Gangplank but specifically refers to the entrance into a ship at head of accommodation ladder.

GARBOARD STRAKE. The plank that fits next to the keel along its full length. In vessels built of modern materials, the turn from bottom to keel is called 'the garboard area'.

GASKETS. Short lengths of line used to secure a furled sail.

GATHER WAY. To start moving through the water with increasing speed.

GEAR. Can refer to any collection of items necessary on a boat.

GEL COAT. The final coat of resin applied to a fibreglass layup after fairing and sanding. Usually is pigmented.

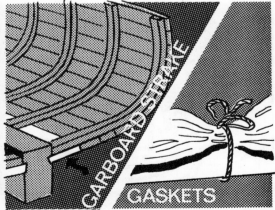

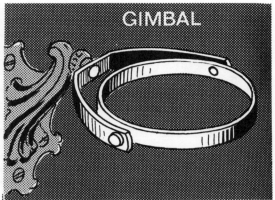

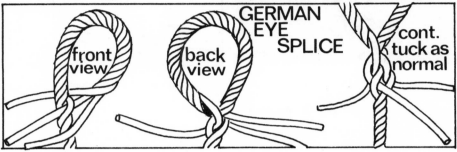

GENOA. A large headsail which overlaps the shrouds.

GERMAN EYE SPLICE. An eye splice where the first strand is tucked with the lay instead of against it.

GIMBALS. A system of hanging a stove, lamp, compass, etc., in such a way that the object remains level regardless of the ship's motion.

GIRTH BAND. A strengthening strip of material sewn from the clew to the luff.

GO ABOUT. Changing from one tack to the other when sailing close hauled.

GOOSENECK. The fitting which secures the boom to the mast allowing it to swing from side to side and to lift and drop.

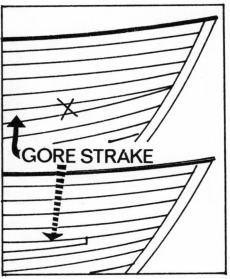

GOOSEWING. Running with the wind using the mainsail and a boomed out headsail on the opposite side. Can also describe a mainsail and mizzen on opposite sides, or twin headsails.

GORE STRAKE. Any plank in the skin of a vessel that tapers to a point before reaching the stem. This is bad practise and such a plank should terminate as shown by the dotted line.

GRAB LINES. The line around a lifeboat which hangs in bights giving a distressed person something to grip prior to being hauled aboard.

GRAB RAIL. The 'handrails' around the top of a cabin.

GRANNY KNOT. An insecure and easily jambed knot. Should not be used aboard ship. The reef knot is the best alternative.

GRAPNEL. An anchor-like object used for blind searching the sea-bed for lost line, chain, etc. Can double as a light weather reef-pick but should not be trusted.

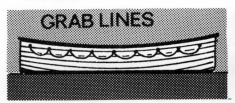

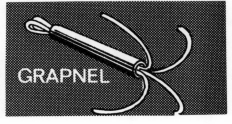

GRASS LINE. See Coir Rope.

GRATING. A lattice-work frame which fits over hatches requiring ventilation. Primarily used on small yachts as a cockpit floor cover.

GRAVING. The act of cleaning a ship's bottom and protecting it with paint. Thus the term 'graving dock'.

GRIPE. The small deadwood uniting keel and stem. Sometimes enlarged to increase forward area's 'bite' in the sea and thus improving lateral resistance.

GRIPES. Webbing straps used to lash a dinghy in davits to prevent it moving.

GRIPING SPAR. A spar covered with pudden fenders placed in such a way that it holds a dinghy away from the davits. Also the traditional place from where a scrambling net is suspended.

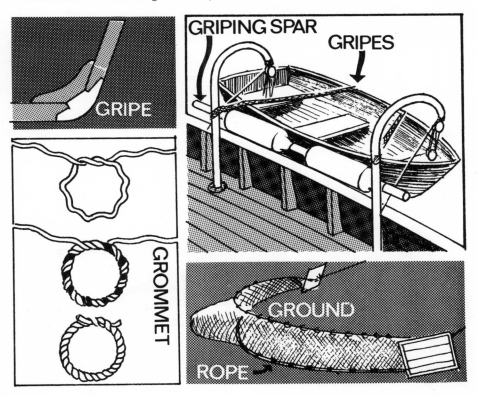

GROMMET. A ring made of one strand of rope laid around itself three times.

GROUND ROPE. The roping along the bottom of a trawl net. Also called the 'lead line' because of the weights attached.

GROUND SWELL. The shorter and sometimes steeper swell experienced over the Continental Shelf.

GROUND TACKLE. Collective term for all anchors and anchor cables aboard ship.

GROWN SPAR. A wooden spar shaped from a single tree.

G.R.P. The abbreviation for Glass Reinforced Plastics. Describes the construction method of any fibreglass vessel. Also called Fibre Reinforced Plastics (F.R.P.).

GUARD RAILS. Safety rails fitted around any open deck.

GUDGEON. The fittings down the sternpost into which the rudder pintles fit.

GUN. The top man in his job. Often used to describe the best fisherman in the fleet. He is the 'gun' fisherman.

GUNTER. A rig which uses a spar similar to a gaff but stands more perpendicular when set.

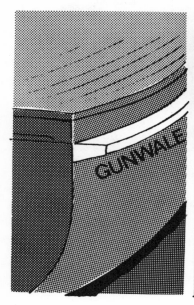

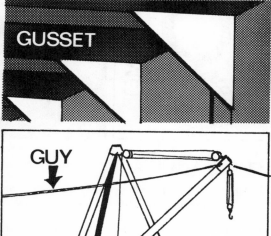

GUNWALE. Originally referred to the covering timber around the deck at deck line to which guns were belayed. Now rather nebulous. Can refer to specific items in the area such as covering board, sheer strake and rubbing strip. Is most commonly used to name the rubbing strip as shown. Also spelt gunwhales and gunnels.

GUSSET. Any plate regardless of material which effectively knits together two bodies.

GUY. The rope or tackles used to control a derrick laterally.

GYBE. When the main boom of a fore and aft rigged vessel sweeps from one side to the other whilst running with the wind. Can be controlled by hauling in the mainsheet as it comes or uncontrolled where, because of inattention or violent seas, the boom crashes across, often damaging rigging or ripping sails.

GYRO COMPASS. A gyroscope electrically driven and aligned with the earth's axis so that it indicates true north. The main unit is mounted well down below decks from where repeaters are fed. The gyro must be adjusted for latitude and ship's speed. Ineffective in latitudes higher than 75 degrees.

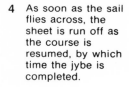

4 As soon as the sail flies across, the sheet is run off as the course is resumed, by which time the jybe is completed.

3 The vessel is turned until the sail is blown back at the top, at which moment it will jybe.

2 The mainsail is sheeted in ready to jybe. The vessel is held on course.

1 Vessel runs with mainsail over starboard side. To jybe, it must be placed over the port side.

WIND

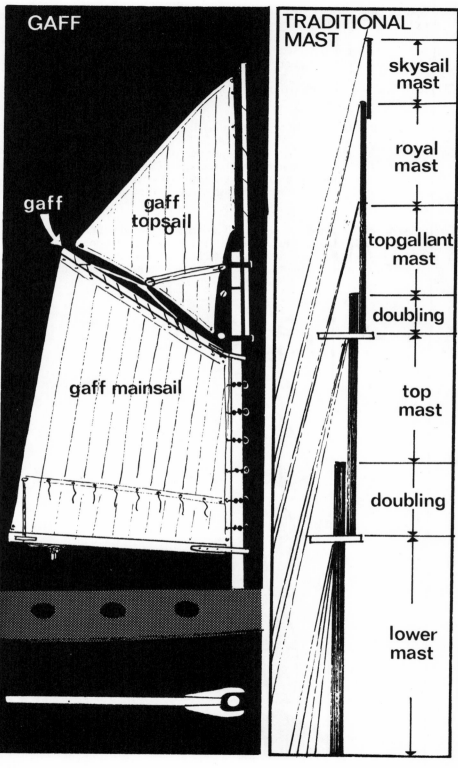

GAFF

gaff

gaff topsail

gaff mainsail

TRADITIONAL MAST

skysail mast

royal mast

topgallant mast

doubling

top mast

doubling

lower mast

Gaff rig occurred quite logically along the
evolutionary path from square rig to the modern
bermudan rig. As can be seen (right) a spar, or 'gaff'
is hoisted aloft under which hangs the mainsail. The
method still has many advantages but its prime reason
for remaining in vogue was the difficulty in finding
mast timber long enough to permit the high aspect
bermudan type to develop. When box section hollow
masts became a reality the gaff rig fell rapidly in
popularity. Below can be seen a close-up of the gaff
jaw with its tumbler and throat halyard connection.
The North Australian pearling luggers (bottom) used
gaff exclusively and although ketch rigged, their sails
were named as if schooner rigged.

Any opening on a horizontal surface which admits cargo or people is called a hatch regardless of its type. Shown here is the forward hatch of a yacht with the lid hinged. The small flap on its after end is a hinged storm board. The lid is held closed with a hasp and staple which is padlocked.

Left: *The winches used for the halyards on this mast are actually sheet winches. A true halyard winch is suitable for wire rope only, the rope being irremovable from the drum.* Below: *This stainless steel horse is used for the mainsheet. Note the rubber cusioned buffers at each end and the traveller-cleat combination. The block at the top of the photograph is a double block made of timber.*

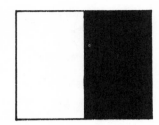

H. Flag of the International Code of Signals meaning 'I have a pilot aboard'. It is white and red in two vertical bars.

HALF BEAM. A beam that is cut to form a hatchway or similar opening.

HALF COWL VENTILATOR. One designed to fit hard against a cabin on deck so as to scoop air without actually presenting a deck obstacle.

HALF HITCH. Made by passing the end of rope through a bight formed as shown.

HALYARDS. Ropes with which sails, flags, spars, etc., are hoisted. Also spelt 'halliards'.

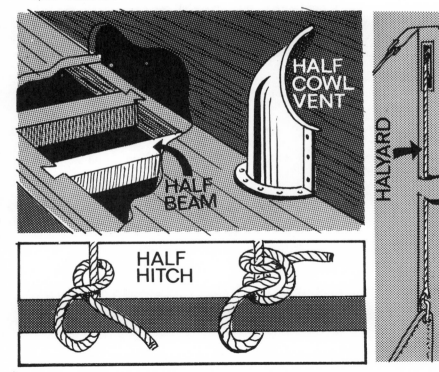

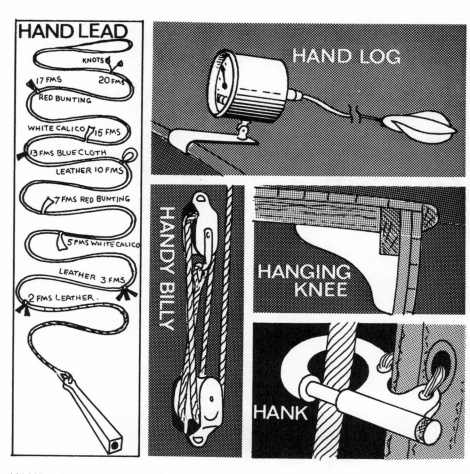

HAND. A crew member, so called because a man is considered as having only one useful working hand aboard ship. The other is 'for the ship' — to hang on with.

HAND A SAIL. To furl a sail.

HAND LEAD. A weighted line for taking depth readings. Traditionally marked as shown in illustration.

HAND LOG. A speed and distance measuring device trailed from the stern. Consists of an impellor on the end of a length of line the other end of which enters the information head.

HANDY BILLY. A small tackle consisting of one single and one double block used around ship for miscellaneous jobs.

HANGING KNEE. A strengthening bracket placed under a deck or cabin.

HANK. The clip used to fasten a headsail onto its stay. There are many forms available, The one shown is a piston hank.

HARD LAID. Said of a rope that has been tightly laid up. Very difficult to splice.

120.

HARD CHINE. A more positive way of naming the chine. *See* Chine *illustration.*

HARD TACK. Said of ship's biscuits and generally used to denote any below average food.

HARPINGS. Thicker or extra planking on forward part of hull topsides. Especially around bow where anchor tends to damage.

HARP PIECE. Definition vague but has been used by native divers to describe the uniting transverse timber across stern of pearling lugger.

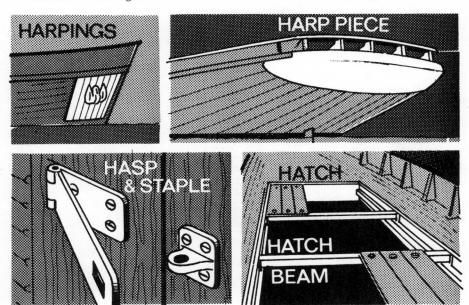

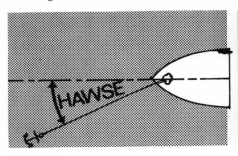 

HASP AND STAPLE. A hatch or door locking device as shown.

HATCH. Opening in deck giving access below.

HATCH BEAMS. Removable members fitted across a cargo hatch to carry the hatch covers.

HATCH COAMING. *See* Coaming.

HAWSE. The angle between anchor line and ship's fore and aft line. Also is angle scribed between the two cables where two anchors are down.

HAWSE BLOCK. Wooden plug shaped to fit into hawse pipe to prevent entry of sea. Not used in modern application.

HAWSE HOLES. The holes on either side of the stem through which anchor cable passes from ship to anchors.

HAWSE PIPE. The tube connecting the hawse hole with cable deck. In small boats the chain pipe is often referred to as the 'hawse pipe'. This is close but, strictly speaking, incorrect.

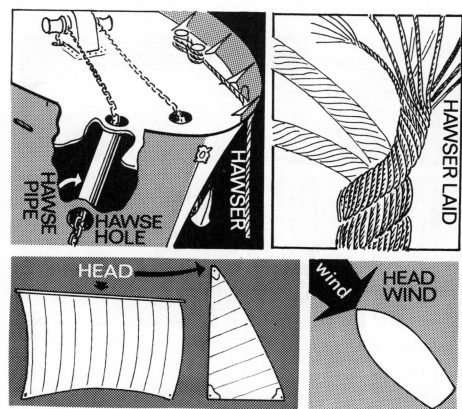

HAWSER. Flexible steel rope or fibre rope used for warping, hauling and mooring.

HAWSER LAID. Rope in which the yarns are spun right handed then laid into strands left handed then the strands are laid up right handed. This is the common method and is distinct from cable lay.

HEAD. The top of a squaresail, the top corner of a triangular sail, a shaped vertical timber. Also refers to the ship's latrines, but is usually spelt in the plural.

HEAD SAILS. Any sail set forward of the foremast.

HEAD SHEETS. 1. Sheets of a head sail. 2. Flooring in forepart of a boat.

HEAD WIND. A wind blowing directly over the bow.

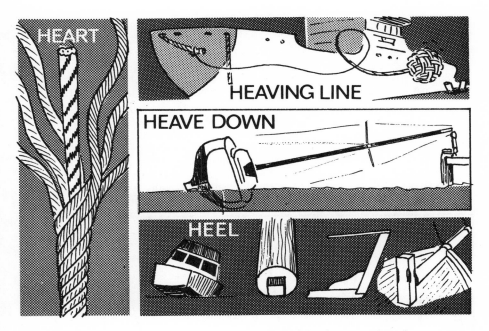

HEART. The centre core in wire rope. Can be soft (fibre) or hard (steel). Soft core is used in flexible steel rope.

HEAVE DOWN. A method of careening a vessel whilst still afloat. All ballast is removed and tackle is attached to the tops of the lower masts to a point ashore.

HEAVING LINE. A small 'messenger' line thrown ahead of a larger line. The larger line is hauled ashore or to the tugboat by the light line.

HEEL. 1. To list under wind pressure or uneven stowage of goods and people. 2. The lower end of a mast. 3. The junction of sternpost and keel. 4. The inboard end of a bowsprit.

Hawse holes and pipes on small ships can be useful. They present a permanent stowage position for the anchor as well as decreasing the angle between cable and sea bottom. The anchor shown is a Dreadnought.

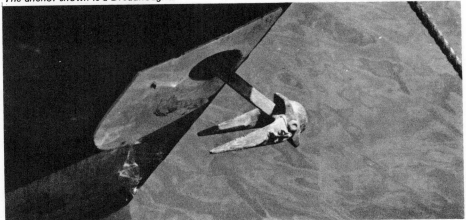

HEELED WATERLINES. The plan view shape of a boat's waterline when heeled.

An important design consideration especially in sailing craft whose performance depends greatly on efficiency when heeled. As the illustrations show, waterlines can change dramatically when heeled, the leeward side bulging out alarmingly and the windward side flattening off.

Three types of basic hulls are shown. Left, is the 'Cod's Head and Mackerel Tail' type which has its greatest beam and buoyancy forward of amidships. Centre, is a 'Symmetrical' hull which has greatest beam and buoyancy amidships. Right, shows the modern 'Wedge' type hull where the greatest beam and buoyancy is aft of amidships. The wedge shape is quite evident in the leeward heeled waterline and whilst rather distorted, this shape actually assists the hull to windward. Generally speaking, however, the symmetrical hull has the least vices under heeling moments.

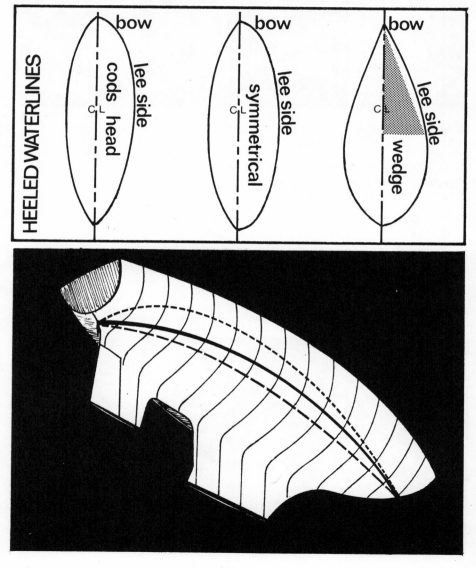

HEELED WATERLINES

bow   bow   bow

cods head   lee side

symmetrical   lee side

wedge   lee side

HEELING ERROR. Compass error due to the redistribution of magnetic forces within the ship when heeled.

HELM. The steering apparatus controlling the rudder, be it wheel or tiller.

HELMSMAN. Person steering a vessel.

HEMP. Cordage made from the hemp plant (usually Indian).

HERMAPHRODITE BRIG. *See* Brigantine.

HIGHFIELD LEVER. An instant tensioning device which holds itself on by the tension it creates. Used extensively on running backstays and variable tensioning backstays.

HIT AND MISS VENTILATOR. A grating behind which slides a mating member which closes and opens the apertures.

HOBBY HORSING. Said of a vessel when rocking violently fore and aft into a head sea.

HOGGED. Refers to a craft that has sagged fore and aft leaving a rise amidships. Commonly occurs to old timber ships, especially if the main shrouds have been too tight.

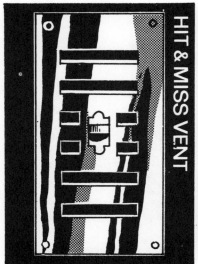

HOLD. The cargo space aboard ship.

HOLDING GROUND. Bottom of sea when the anchor will grip.

HOOK. Slang for 'anchor'.

HOOKER. Term of endearment or derision for a vessel.

HORN TIMBER. The timber joining the sternpost to the transom.

HORSE. 1. Bar along which the sheet of a fore and aft sail traverses. Thus, the 'mainhorse' or the 'staysail horse'. 2. The footrope beneath the yard supporting crewmen. *See* Footrope.

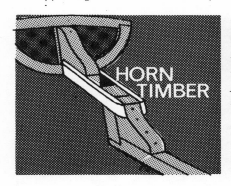
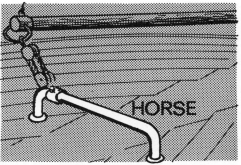

HORSE LATITUDES. Calm areas between trade wind belt and the westerlies of higher latitudes. Generally between 30 to 35 degrees. So named, presumably, because of the number of fatalities amongst cavalry horses en route to British Colonies whilst the ship lay becalmed.

HORSING. Caulking the seams in a ship's side planking.

HOUNDS. Shoulders formed by reducing the thickness of a mast which support shrouds and stays or can support a whole structure of trestle trees and cross trees.

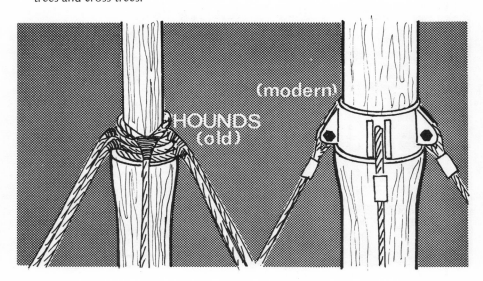

HOVERCRAFT. A vessel which lifts above the sea by the downward pressure of air created by propellers. The forward and reverse motion is similarly created.

HOVE TO. Lying nearly head to wind. Not moving but maintaining station by control of sails or engine.

HULL. The body of a vessel.

HULL DOWN. Said of a ship when the hull is below horizon leaving only superstructure visible.

HURRICANE. Force 12 on the Beaufort Scale. 64 to 71 knots winds. More generally used to describe destructive winds in certain parts of the world well above those speeds.

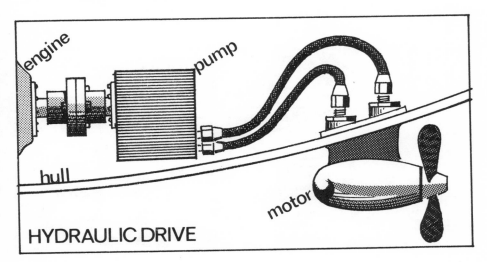

HYDRAULIC DRIVE. A method of propulsion utilising the hydraulic
system. The engine, be it diesel, petrol or whatever, couples directly to
an oil pump which delivers oil at high pressure into a motor.
The propellor is attached to this motor. The motor can be part of the
propellor bearing housing, as shown, or can be inside the vessel at the end
of a conventional propellor shaft. If the former, units of low power
range only can be used.

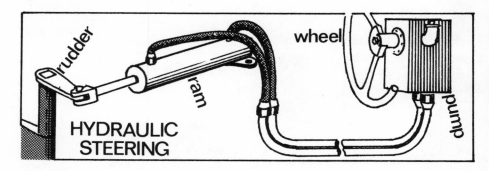

HYDRAULIC STEERING. A system employing a wheel operated motor
which activates a ram onto the rudder head. The system offers versatility
in that copper pipes replace cables, bevel gears, pulleys, etc. Its major
drawback is insensitivity. A helmsman seldom feels any response from a
sea against the rudder and seven or eight turns from lock to lock is not
uncommon giving the helsman easy, but consistent, work.

HYDROFOIL. A vessel which lifts bodily out of the water at high speed to be
borne on underwater wings. The type was actually proposed as far back
as 1869. Italian inventor, Enrico Forlanini successfully tested a hydrofoil
on Lake Maggiore in Switzerland in 1905. In later years many eminent
inventors, including Alexander Graham Bell and the Wright brothers,
experimented with the type. Because of the weight of machinery in those
days, the vessels tended to be too heavy and impractical.. With the advent
of World War II, the type forged ahead. It is now commonly used as
a passenger ferry and was first introduced into Australia on the
Manly-Sydney run during the early 1960's.

The word 'gale' is just a word to most people. To others it is a sentence. The death sentence. The finish of a fine ship. The bow section of the giant ore carrier, Sygna broke free on a beach on the New South Wales coast, Australia, during a gale in 1974 and was later towed into harbour. The stern section was a total loss. Dugong, a Hartley designed Tasman ferro-cement yacht, fetched the beach along the same coast during a gale in June 1976. She was eventually salvaged suffering only the loss of one bilge keel and a few hairline cracks.

1. Whether a small private landing or a main harbour wharf, a structure like this can, with equal accuracy, be called a jetty, wharf, pier or dock although jetty and wharf are the most common names. 2. This sail hanging from a yard under the bowsprit is called a 'Jimmy Green'. 3. Junks have a high poop deck which commonly overhangs the transom. 4. On any size vessel a ladder up the mast — called the Jacob's Ladder, is a must. It is a means of gaining vision when making a landfall or for maintaining the mast properly. 5. 'Leading Beacons' are shown here. When the two are kept in line the best water is found through shoal areas. 6. This chine hull has two 'corners' at the bilge making her a 'multi chine' type. 7. Lifebuoys are traditionally a ring of floatation. Nowadays foam sandwich fibreglass predominates. 8. A typical folding propellor. Centrifugal force throws it open when the engine is run.

Impellor Pump

The direction of rotation and the principle of collapsing chambers is clearly shown in the illustration bottom right.

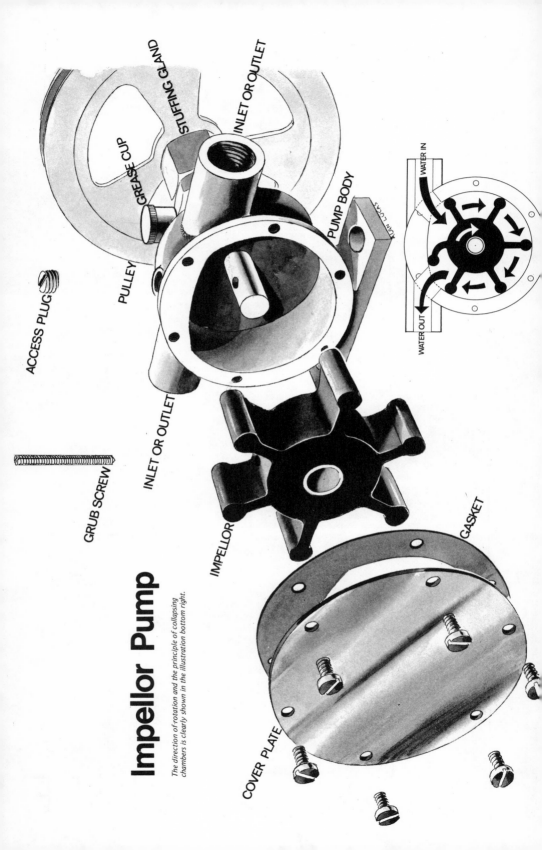

GREASE CUP

STUFFING GLAND

INLET OR OUTLET

PULLEY

PUMP BODY

ACCESS PLUG

WATER IN

WATER OUT

INLET OR OUTLET

GRUB SCREW

IMPELLOR

GASKET

COVER PLATE

I. Flag of the International Code of Signals. Means 'I am altering my course to port'. It is yellow with a black circle.

IMPELLOR PUMP. A fully rotating pump which depends on the collapse and expansion of chambers between the blades of a synthetic impellor to create a sucking and expelling action. This type is ideal on the small ship for all motor driven pumps especially in engine cooling. It cannot successfully be operated by hand. The impellor, being the only moving part, usually ends its useful life by breaking at the base of the blades. It should be replaced at this stage. The life span depends on use but with moderate revolutions per minute, pumping only clear, clean water, many years trouble free running can be expected. Details will be found in the full-page exploded view illustration.

IN BALLAST. Said of any vessel when not carrying cargo. In this state it is normal to lower the centre of gravity by loading ballast. In sailing ship days the ballast was usually rock (many harbour breakwaters around the world are partly or totally constructed from ship's ballast). Modern ships use sea water admitted to baffled tanks.

INBOARD ENGINE. The engine of a boat which is placed inboard and drives the craft by a standard arrangement of propellor shaft and propellor which are not integral with the engine construction.

INBOARD-OUTBOARD. A transom mounted unit consisting of engine, transmission and propellor. The drive is transferred down a 'Z' leg to the propellor. The leg has similar characteristics to an outboard engine in that it lifts to reduce draught. An inboard-outboard unit can only be mounted on a vessel with maximum beat at the stern. It is not suited to yachts and normal displacement launches. Sometimes called a 'Z' drive.

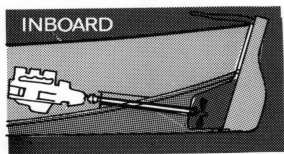 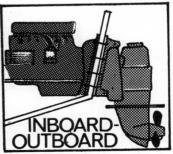

INBOARD

INBOARD-OUTBOARD

133.

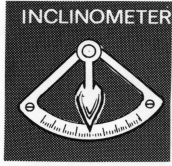

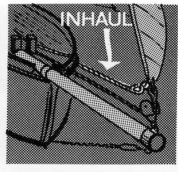

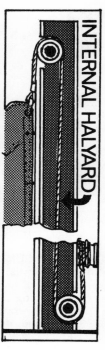

INCLINOMETER. A pendulum and pointer which swings across a graduated scale showing the angle of heel (when placed athwartships) or the pitching angle (when placed fore and aft).

INHAUL. Any rope used to bring a sail or spar inboard. Typically, the flying jib must be inhauled from the end of the bowsprit as shown.

IN IRONS. A sailing vessel with her head to wind and refusing to fall off onto either tack is said to be 'in irons'. To get her moving again she must be 'boxhauled'. This seldom happens to the modern short-keeled yacht.

INSPECTION PORT. A plastic rim and hatch united by a bayonet or part-thread system. Used specifically on sailing skiffs where access through watertight bulkheads is required.

IN STAYS. The position of a sailing vessel when going from one tack to the other whilst her head is to wind.

INTERNAL HALYARD. Any halyard which passes through the mast instead of hanging outside. An innovation made possible by the recent use of aluminium masts. An internal halyard reduces wind resistance and gives a vessel a less cluttered appearance but can be very noisy for anyone trying to sleep below.

INTERNATIONAL CODE. System of flag and morse signals for communication between ships and ship and shore. Last revised in 1964.

IRISH PENDANT. Specifically a frayed flag or pendant, applies to any loose rope-end flying in the breeze and making a vessel look untidy.

IRONBOUND. A rugged coastline offering no landing for small boats.

J. Flag of the International Code of Signals meaning, 'I am on fire and have dangerous cargo on board: keep well clear of me'. It has three horizontal bars blue, white and blue.

JACKASS RIG. This can refer to any unusual combination of masts or sails. Specifically it describes the rig of a four masted barque with two masts rigged square and two masts rigged fore and aft as shown. Typical of the confusing and often baseless jargon used to describe rigs of old, this type can also be called a 'brig-schooner'. Another specific type of jackass rig is the three masted jackass barque said to have been a very handy rig. This was also known as the 'jigger-barque'.

JACKASS RIG

.JACKROPE. The lacing used to bend the foot of a mainsail to the boom.

JACKSTAFF. Small staff on bow on which the jack or other flag is flown.

JACKSTAY. Any rod, batten or wire stretched between two points for a specific purpose such as a wire to which a squaresail is made fast on the yard.

JACK TAR. Nickname for a seaman whose knowledge of his trade is very low.

JACKYARD TOPSAIL. Similar to a club topsail as described under that heading.

JACOB'S LADDER. A ladder used for climbing aboard or aloft.

JAMB CLEAT. One that jambs the rope in a taper.

JAMIE (OR JIMMY) GREEN. A squaresail set under the bowsprit. Used during the clipper ship era.

JAWS. The forked end of a gaff which engages the mast. See gaff illustration.

JAW ROPE. Alternate name for Parrel.

JET ENGINE. A high speed, motor driven pump which circulates sea water at such a rate that forward motion is achieved. Its prime advantage lies in the fact that a hull of shallow draught and obstruction-free underwater profile is possible.

JETTY. A pier or wharf for the use of shipping.

JIB. The foremost sails set between the masthead and the bowsprit. As many as three jibs were set by sailing ships and were known as 'flying jib', 'outer jib' and 'inner jib'. The word jib is often used contemporarily to describe any triangular headsail.

JIB BOOM. The spar projecting forward from the bow to which all jib tacks are fastened.

JIB DOWNHAUL. A rope taken from the top (head) of a jib, through a block at the tack and back to the deck from where it can be pulled to assist in dropping the jib.

JIB FURLING GEAR. A recent innovation used to furl the jib around its stay. Consists of a swivel at the top and a rope-operated reel at the bottom. Works like a roller blind. *See* Roller Furling.

JIB IRON. An iron hoop which travels along the bowsprit and to which a flying jib is set.

JIB OF JIBS. The outermost jib where three or more are carried. Called 'flying jib' if not hanked to a stay.

JIB OUTHAUL. The rope by which the tack of a jib is hauled out along the jib-boom. Typically, it would haul out the jib iron with sail attached.

JIB SHEET. *See* Sheet.

JIB STAY. The stay to which the jib is hanked. *See* Forestay.

JIGGER. Alternative name for 'spanker' or 'driver' on a square rigged ship. 2. Alternative name for Handybilly.

JIFFY REEFING. A quick method of reefing a mainsail employing permanently reeved tack and clew lines as shown. Basically it is identical to common slab reefing. At the tack (leading) end of the sail a line is fixed to one side of the mast, through the tack reef cringle and down to the mast on the opposite where it passes loosely through a cheek block or deadeye to a cleat. Similarly, at the other end of the boom a line is taken from one side of the boom, through the clew reef cringle and back down to the boom on the opposite side where it, too, passes through a block or deadeye to a cleat. To reef, the halyard is slackened off to a predetermined point and the tack and clew lines are hauled in and belayed. Lines permanently established in reef cringles along the foot of the sail are then tied around the excess sail and boom.

JOGGLED FRAME. A frame having alternate raised and recessed portions to permit rivetted plating to lie hard against the frame at all points whilst overlapping each other. The joggled frame is not used in modern all-welded ships.

JUNIOR OFFSHORE GROUP. An English born club formed to organise and conduct races for small yachts. Vessels of waterline length not more than 23 feet (7 metres) are eligible. The first Australian branch was formed in Sydney in 1958.

JUMPER STAY. *See* Triatic Stay.

JUNK. A Chinese sailing ship with one or more masts. Commonly three masts are carried and the sails are fully battened.

JURY MAST. Any temporary replacement for the vessel's mast or masts which have carried away.

JURY RIG. The temporary stays and shrouds used to support a jury mast.

JURY RUDDER. A temporary steering arrangement when the rudder has been rendered useless. Commonly the floorboards are used. On some vessels control can be gained by balancing the sails so that little steerage is required and the course is kept by trailing an iron bucket astern to one side or the other as demanded.

JIGGER

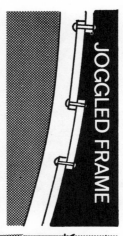

JOGGLED FRAME

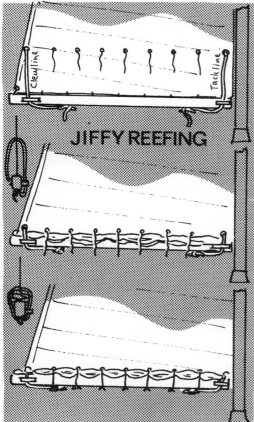

JIFFY REEFING

JUNK

JURY MAST

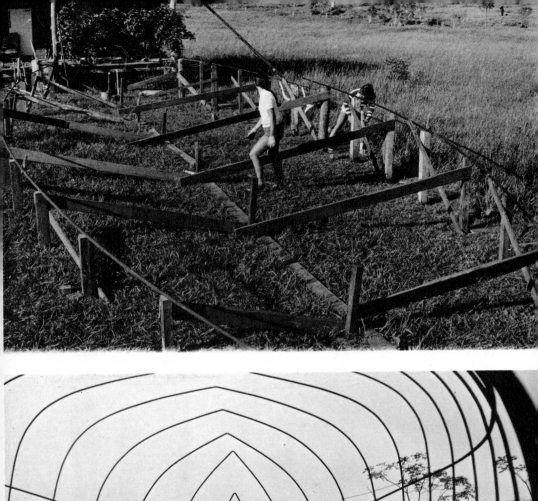

4

1. When the frames of a hull are lofted full size, the next step
is to set out the base on which the frames sit. This is the deck
plan of a Wilf O'Kell design ferro-cement schooner. 2. When
the sheerline is established, frames are erected at regular
intervals or 'stations'. 3. A pontoon with a hinged ramp to
shore represents the best type of boat landing because it
remains a constant height from the water. 4. A simple but
effective pulpit protects the bow of this yacht. This also
shows a good example of a laid deck. 5. 'Paddling' describes
the act of propelling a boat with a single shaft paddle, even if
that paddle is in fact a spinnaker pole! 6. The rail around the
stern of this yacht can be called a 'pulpit'. Modern
terminology has called it the 'pushpit'.

5

6

Above: *A fine example of a motor-sailer. This type depends as much on power as it does on sail being reasonably efficient in both fields. Large deckhouses and centre cockpits are typical of the type. Note the external shroud, or chain, plates.* Left: *A Chinese Junk. This is an abandoned private craft.* Below: *Designer and builder discuss the construction of the stem area of a ferro-cement boat. Although the word 'stem' describes the piece of timber in that area, the term applies now to whatever replaces timber in modern materials.*

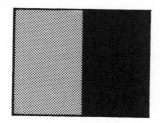

K. Flag of the International Code of Signals meaning, 'I wish to communicate with you.' It has two vertical bands, yellow and blue.

KATABATIC. The downward flow of air when due to convection. Typically, when wind blows down from a mountain onto low land because of the hotter air rising from the latter.

KEDGE ANCHOR. An anchor used to 'kedge' a vessel from one position to another. Any type of anchor might be used but normally the Admiralty Pattern is chosen for its maximum holding and ease of breaking out. Usually two anchors and cables are employed, one being carried ahead by the long boat as the other is coming aboard.

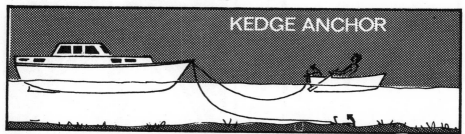

KEEL. The 'backbone' of any ship. It lies fore and aft along the centreline of the bottom.

KEEL DOUBLER. A full length member fastened directly to the keel which is slightly wider to form a ledge on which the garboard strakes land. This is an alternative method of construction to using a one piece keel with its sides rabbeted for the strakes. It is sometimes called the 'keelson'.

KEELER. Nickname of man employed on a keel craft. Nowadays is used to identify any deep keeled vessel as against a multi hull or motor boat. 2. Tub used to hold caulking material.

KEEL HAULING. Punishment used in olden days. An offender was hauled under the ship from one side to another by a line from one end of a yard to the other.

KEELSON. An inner keel laid along the top of the floors and through-bolted to the keel. Sometimes the keel doubler is referred to as the keelson.

KEELSON TOPPING. A mating length of timber laid directly onto the keelson for added strength.

KETCH. Sailing vessel with fore and aft rig on two masts, the after mast (mizzen) being shorter than the main mast and stepped forward of the rudder. This tends to be the most popular cruising rig because of the ease of sail change and balance.

KEVEL HEAD. Projection of a rib above the deck which is used as a bitt.

KILLICK. General name for an anchor; originally a stone used for same.

KINETIC ENERGY. Energy due to motion. For example, the energy created by a piston rushing in either direction.

KING PLANK. The centre plank along any deck.

KING POST. Alternative name for 'sampson post'.

KING SPOKE. A specially marked spoke in the steering wheel which indicates midship position. A valuable reference point for the helmsman.

KNEE. A timber or steel member which unites two other structural members. Sometimes called a 'hook'. Typical application is in uniting and strengthening the ship's sides to her decks (hanging knee) and the stringers to each other and to the stem (lateral or breast knee or hook). *See* Breast Hook *and* Hanging Knee *illustrations.*

KNIGHT HEADS. Two strong timbers extending upwards from each side of the stem and between which the bowsprit passes.

KNOT. Nautical unit of velocity used internationally regardless of national measurement system. It is 6,080 feet per hour. Because the knot is a complete statement it is unnecessary and incorrect to state a speed as so many 'knots per hour'.

KURALON. Old name for 'Vinylon'. This is the synthetic equivalent of cotton rope which it has largely replaced. It is of the Polyvinyl Alcohol family and has a large degree of stretch. It is much stronger and more abrasion resistant than its natural counterpart but will lose strength after prolonged exposure to sunlight.

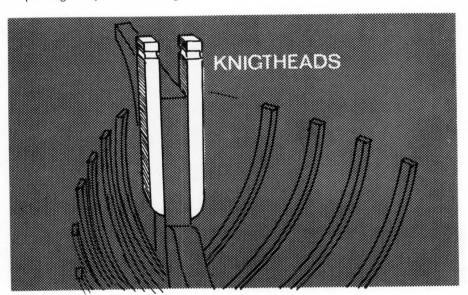

KNIGTHEADS

L. Flag of the International Code of Signals, means, 'You should stop your vessel instantly'. Coloured yellow and black.

LABOUR. A vessel is said to be 'labouring' when making little headway through big seas.

LACING. Small line used to lace sails to booms, dodgers to rails, etc.

LADING. The cargo.

LAG BOLT. Alternative name for Coach Screw.

LAGGING. A non-conductive wrapping around boilers, exhaust pipes, etc. Usually asbestos rope.

LAID DECK. A traditional type of deck where planks are laid and caulked between.

LANDFALL. Bringing the land up after an ocean passage. 'Making a landfall'.

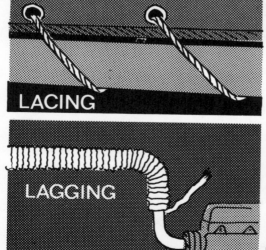

LACING

LAGGING

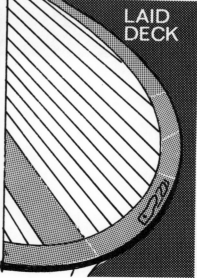

LAID DECK

LANDING. The overlap of planks or plates.

LANDING STRAKE. The second strake, or plank, below the gunwale.

LANDLUBBER. A man who knows little of the sea.

LANDMARK. Any conspicuous object ashore used as an identifying point.

LANDS. The overlaps in the planking of a clinker built boat.

LAND WIND. A wind which blows offshore. Usually caused by warm air rising off the sea after dark during periods of fairly calm weather.

LANG'S LAY. A wire rope where both the wires in the strands and the strands themselves are laid right handed. The disposition of the wires in Lang's lay rope exposes a greater length of wire to wear and it consequently lasts longer in working conditions. However, because the lay is not self supporting, both ends of the rope, or the weight it is lifting, must be secured against rotation. It is not a rope recommended for general boat work. The illustration shows the normal 'right hand regular lay' rope and Lang's lay.

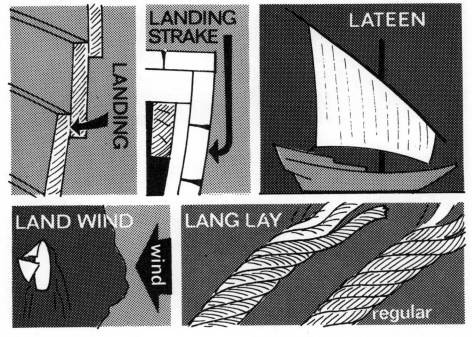

LANYARD. Short length of line used for securing objects.

LAPSTRAKE. An alternative name for 'Clinker Built'.

LARBOARD. Obsolete name for 'port' which is the left-hand side of the boat. Believed to have developed from the words, 'land side' (land board) from when ships coming home to England brought up the land on the left-hand side. Changed to 'port' to avoid confusion with 'starboard'.

LATEEN SAIL. A triangular sail with a long inclined luff which is laced to a yard. The leech is vertical. Used extensively in eastern countries.

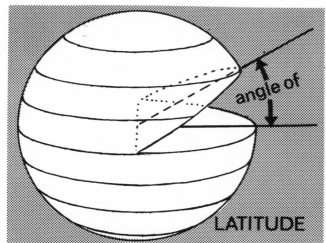

angle of

LATITUDE

LEAD

LATERAL RESISTANCE

lateral force (wind)

lateral resistance (water)

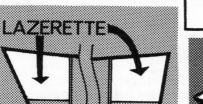

LAZERETTE

LAUNCH

LATEEN YARD. The long spar to which the lateen sail is bent. *See* Lateen Sail *illustration.*

LATERAL RESISTANCE. The resistance of a hull to being driven sideways. The resistance increases with the rate of travel and the rate of travel can effectively be reduced by designing keels short and deep rather than long and shallow. Racing rules and practical common sense deny the rise of excessively deep keels but a happy medium of a moderately deep, short keel in conjunction with a separate skeg-rudder combination has produced a sailing hull which is very efficient to windward. Power boats, because of their mechanical means of propulsion, do not have, nor do they need to have, the same degree of lateral resistance as a sailing boat. *See* Centre of Lateral Resistance.

LATITUDE. The distance from equator measured as an angle at the centre of the earth from the equatorial plane.

LAUNCH. To move a vessel into the water from the builder's yard.
2. An open or half decked boat. Generally extended to include cabin boats. Thus, 'half cabin launch', 'full cabin launch' or 'open launch'.

LAY. The direction strands of a rope are 'laid'. Thus right handed or left handed rope. *See also* Lang's Lay.

LAY UP. The transferring of measurements from the offset table of a hull plan to full size on the lofting floor.

LAZARETTE. A stowage area either right forward or right aft. Is often incorrectly used to denote stowage space aft only.

LAZYJACKS. Lines from the gaff to the boom on gaff rigged vessels which confine the sail as it drops.

LEAD. (Pronounced leed) The direction in which a rope goes after passing through a block. (Pronounced led). A shaped lead weight weighing around 14 lb attached to the end of a marked line used to ascertain the depth of water by casting the lead and reading off the marked line. Collectively known as 'lead line'.

LEADING BEACONS

LEADING BEACONS. Two beacons which, when kept in line (in transit) will hold the ship's course clear of shoal water. Usually triangular, the back-lead being inverted, but can be oblong with a painted shape on the board.

LEADING CLEAT. An open based cleat, as shown, used for leading a rope through before cleating. Can also be used as a fairlead alone.

LEAD MINE. Mostly used derogatively, describes a narrow beamed vessel of deep draught requiring considerable weight of ballast to maintain stability.

LEE. The area sheltered from the wind. Refers to the side of the vessel sheltered from the wind.

LEE BOARD. An external 'centre board' fitted to each side of a shallow draught hull to increase lateral resistance and thus decrease leeway.

A properly fitted leeboard can be 'cocked' in such a way that it helps steer the vessel upwind. The leeboard's basic advantage lies in its accessibility for maintenance and repair and it represents the most efficient type of drop-keel available. 2. A board fitted along the edge of a bunk to prevent the occupant falling out when the vessel is heeled.

LEECH. The after edge of a fore and aft sail. Both edges of a squaresail designated as fore and after leech depending on which is to windward. Sometimes spelt 'leach'. *See illustration opposite* Sail.

LEE HELM. When the tiller is to leeward to keep the bow up to wind. Usually caused by too much sail forward. Not desirable for efficient sailing.

LEE HELMSMAN. Where the person steering a vessel sits downwind of the wheel or tiller.

LEE LURCH. Said when a vessel is thrown to leeward (*away* from the wind) by a combination of wind and wave conditions.

LEE-O. An order meaning 'we are going about' (tacking).

LEE SHORE. A shore onto which the wind is blowing and is thus under the lee of an offshore vessel.

LEE SIDE. That side of the vessel or object that is sheltered from the wind.

LEE TIDE. When the tidal flow runs in the same direction as the wind.

LEEWARD. The direction in which the wind blows.

LEEWAY. The sideways travel of a vessel when effected by wind. It is referred to as the angle between the intended course and the actual course after leeway is considered.

LET FLY. Order to suddenly free sheets so that the sail or sails will instantly spill their wind.

LIE TO. To stop a vessel and let her lie to the prevailing conditions with her head towards the wind.

LIFE BELT. A canvas or synthetic belt or jacket filled with buoyancy material and worn to support a person in the water.

LIFEBOAT. Open boats or launches fitted to davits aboard ship or housed ashore for the sole purpose of carrying survivors from a distressed ship.

LIFEBUOY. A ring or horseshoe shaped buoyant apparatus capable of supporting a person in the water. Originally canvas covered cork. Now foam sandwich.

LIE TO

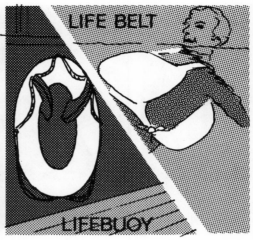

LIFE BELT

LIFEBOAT

LIFEBUOY

LIFTING EYE CLEAT. As shown, a cleat and eye in one.

LIFTS. Lines from mast to ends of yard to support, lift and acockbill the yard.

LIGHTER. A barge without means of propulsion. Originally used to take excess cargo from a vessel wanting to enter shallow water and thus lighten her.

LIGHTSHIP. A vessel permanently anchored in the one place displaying a navigational light. Usually has no means of propulsion. The name is often given to a lighthouse service ship which is in every way a self propelled ship, fully manned and employed solely to maintain and service lighthouses along a coast.

LIGNUM VITAE. A hard timber used for external propellor shaft bearings and deadeyes.

LIFTING EYE CLEAT

LIGHTER

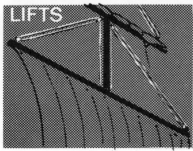

LIFTS

LIGHTSHIP

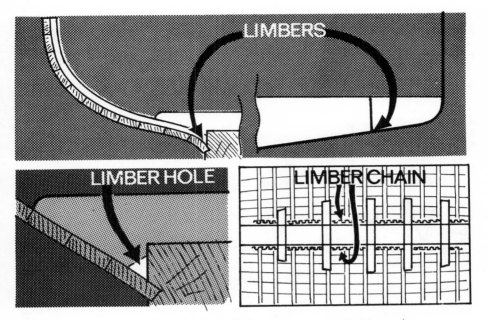

LIMBER. The channel down each side of the keelson on small ships and the tanks of large ships.

LIMBER CHAIN. A chain threaded through limber holes in the floors to clear them of debris.

LIMBER HOLES. The holes cut in the floors to prevent bilge water collecting in any one area.

LIST. To lean one way or the other.

LIZARD. A rope or wire pendant with a round thimble at one end through which a line can be led.

LOADLINE. *See* Plimsoll Line.

LOCK. Part of a canal (artificial waterway) which can be closed off by gates and the water therein raised or lowered.

LOCKER. A 'cupboard' in a boat.

LOCKER RING. A loose fitting ring trapped in a flush plate used for opening lockers and, primarily, hatches where a non-fouling handle is required.

LOFT. A large flat floor area used to mark out sails or the full size frames of a hull.

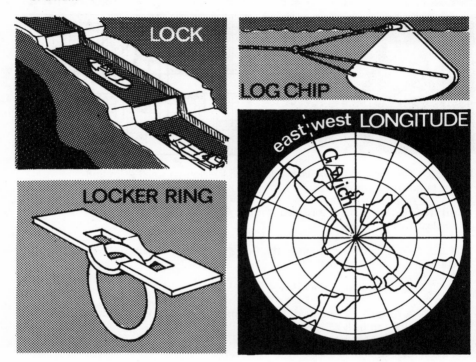

LOG. An apparatus trailed astern to ascertain speed and distance. Comes from ancient method of casting a piece of timber (log) overside then counting and timing the number of knots in the attached line as they sped out. Now such devices as the Walkers Patent Log are used which consist of an information head (dial) fixed to the stern rail which is activated by a logline trailed aft at the end of which is an impellor which slowly rotates. *See also* Sum Log *and* Hand Log

LOG BOOK. Journal of shipboard events.

LOG CHIP. A quadrant shaped piece of timber ballasted on the curved end and attached to a towing line by a bridle. Used to ascertain ship's speed as described under heading 'log'. Is hauled aboard by jerking a pin out which releases one line of the bridle. Also called 'logship'.

LONG BOAT. Formerly the largest boat carried by a merchant ship.

LONGITUDE. The position on earth of any place measured in degrees east or west of Greenwich.

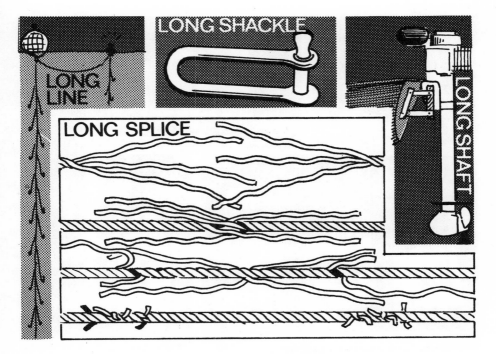

LONG LINE. A single fishing line with dozens or hundreds of hooks
attached on short lines down its length. Used extensively by the Japanese
all over the world outside the continental shelf of various countries. The
more sophisticated lines are interconnected and suspended by radio buoys
which emit a signal to a master-station aboard ship signifying that a line
has fish attached.

LONG SHACKLE. A special purpose shackle longer than normal.

LONG SHAFT. Said of an outboard motor with an extended 'leg' to permit
the motor to be hung on transoms which would otherwise hold the
propellor above the water. Used as auxiliaries on small yachts etc.

LONG SPLICE. A splice that can run through a block whilst successfully
joining two ends of ropes together. Strands of each end displace their
opposite number and are finished by a half knot.

LOOM. The inboard end of an oar. 2. The light reflected in the sky above
its source. Large towns and cities can be located from sea well ahead of
their actual sighting by the loom. Over large cities the loom can be
visible for over 70 miles.

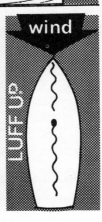

LOOSE FOOTED. A sail not laced to its boom. Suitable light weather arrangement.

LOP. Small, fast sloppy sea.

LOWER BOOM. The same as 'boat boom', described under that heading.

LOWER MAST. Describes the principal mast in a two or three part structure.

LUBBER LINE. The line in the compass to which all course readings relate.

LUFF. The leading edge of a fore and aft sail.

LUFF UP. Order meaning to point the luff of the sail into the wind. Exactly the same as being told to point the bow of the vessel into the wind.

LUGGER. Traditionally a vessel rigged with lugsails. Has been extended to refer to almost any working sail boat regardless of its rig. A typical example is the North Australian pearling lugger which has never been lugsail rigged although it has always carried gaff which is a close relation to the lugsail. As a matter of interest, the ketch rigged luggers mentioned have their sails named as if schooner rigged. An anomaly believed to have been brought about by the original mother ships which were mostly schooner rigged and the natives, manning the luggers, adopted the sail names.

LUGSAIL. A four sided sail hung from a yard which fastens to the mast one third of its length from forward. *See also* Dipping Lug.

LYING TO. The same as 'lie to'.

Above: *The bowsprit of a North Australian Pearling Lugger. The forestay and bobstay meet at the bowsprit collar, which is normal practise. Unusual is the 'second' bobstay which is in fact a continuation of a second 'inner' forestay. Its purpose is to allow the headsail to drop free on its stay all the way down to the bowsprit itself.* Right: *Building the skeg of a ferro-cement boat. The rudder will hang behind it.* Below: *This is a good example of a 'rail'. This one is polished timber sitting atop stainless steel staunchions which in turn are mounted on the toerail capping.*

M. Flag of the International Code of Signals meaning, 'My vessel is stopped and making no way through the water'. Blue with a white cross.

MACKEREL SKY. Fairly orderly bands of cirrocumulus and altocumulus cloud across the sky.

MADE MAST. *See* Built Mast.

MAGNETIC BEARING. The bearing of an object related to the magnetic compass. *See* Cross Bearing *and* Cocked Hat.

MAGNETIC COMPASS. A compass which works on magnetic principles. It is the original type and still the most popular on small boats.

MAGNUS HITCH. A Clove Hitch with an extra turn as shown. Ideal non-slipping hitch where a spar or shroud is used as a securing point.

MAGNUS
HITCH

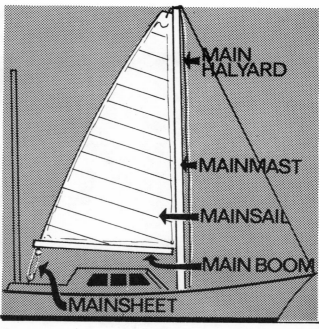

←MAIN HALYARD

←MAINMAST

←MAINSAIL

←MAIN BOOM

←MAINSHEET

MAIN BOOM. The boom used by the mainsail.

MAIN HALYARD. The rope used to hoist the mainsail.

MAINMAST. The principle mast in a multi masted vessel.

MAINRAIL. The bulwark capping. *See* Margin Plank *illustration.*

MAINSAIL. The principle sail. On fore and aft rigged vessels it is always
the largest sail bent on behind the mainmast. On square rigged ships
it is the one from the mainyard.

MAIN SHEET. The rope used to control the mainsail.

MAIN SHEET TRAVELLER. A sophisticated form of 'horse' which
permits the main sheet to travel from one side of the boat to the other
to prevent the sail griping.

MAKE AND MEND. A half day off for seamen to mend clothes.

MAKE FAST. To secure to a jetty or mooring.

MAKE SAIL. To set sail or to increase sail already set.

MAKE WATER. To leak.

MAKING. A rising tide.

MAKING IRON. A large caulking iron used for final hardening up of oakum.

MANGANESE BRONZE. A popular alloy of copper, zinc and manganese
used for boat hardware and fastenings. Although long lasting and
trouble free, fastenings in the material readily break if not
of adequate thickness.

MANILA. *Musa Textilis.* This fibre is a native of the Philippine Islands
and closely resembles the banana plant. The fibre is embedded in the
sheath-like leaf stalks. It entered world trade as a rope making fibre
early in the nineteenth century and quickly established itself as being
the best. It lost favour as a yacht rope in the early 1960's under the
onslaught of synthetic ropes which tended to be at least twice as
strong as manila.

MANROPE. A short length of rope used to assist a person onto a ladder, etc.

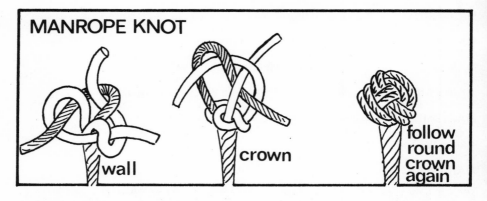

MANROPE KNOT

wall · crown · follow round crown again

MANROPE KNOT. A fancy knot in the end of a manrope whose purpose is to give a secure handhold. It is formed by making a wall knot then crowning it.

MARCONI RIG. An alternative name for bermuda rig but can sometimes specifically describe a particularly slender and tall rig when it resembles a radio mast (thus the name Marconi).

MARE'S TAILS. Wisps of cirrus clouds. Often foretell rain if the cirrus thickens.

MARGIN PLANK. The outside deck plank or strake. In simple small boat construction it lies alongside the covering board and has no identity of its own. In traditional big ship construction it lies alongside the waterway as shown and usually rises at its outer edge.

MARLINE. Two strands of hemp loosely laid up left handed. Used for serving, seizing, etc. Often spelt 'marlin'.

MARLINE HITCH. Made as shown is used to bend sails to spars, etc.

MARLINE SPIKE HITCH. Used to gain purchase with a marline spike.

MARLING. To bind or frap (marl) two objects together.

MARLINE SPIKE HITCH · MARGIN PLANK

MARINER. A person employed aboard ship.

MARINE ENGINE. An engine, either diesel or petrol, identical in character to any other type except for a few extras demanded by the marine environment such as water cooled exhaust manifold, heat exchange cooling system, and, possibly, an oil cooler of some type.

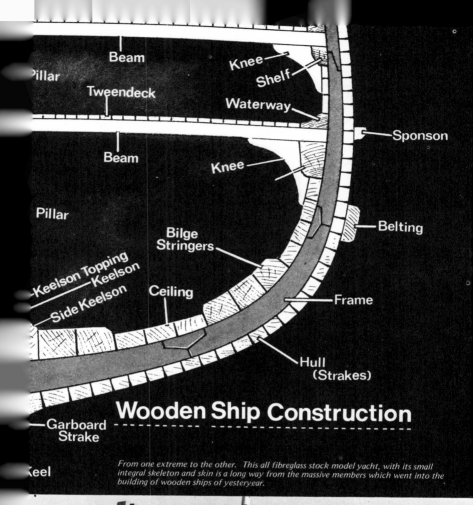

Beam

Pillar

Tweendeck

Beam

Pillar

Knee

Shelf

Waterway

Knee

Sponson

Belting

Bilge
Stringers

Keelson Topping
Keelson

Side Keelson

Ceiling

Frame

Hull
(Strakes)

Wooden Ship Construction

Garboard
Strake

Keel

From one extreme to the other. This all fibreglass stock model yacht, with its small integral skeleton and skin is a long way from the massive members which went into the building of wooden ships of yesteryear.

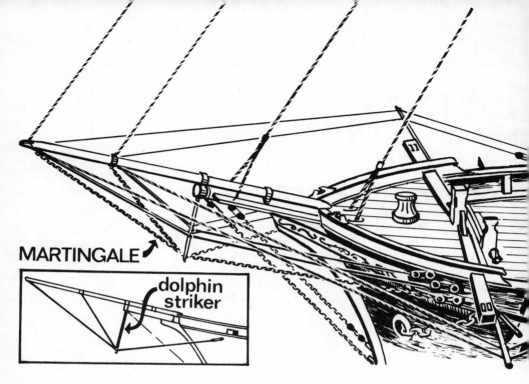

MARTINGALE

dolphin
striker

MARTINGALE. A stay running along the underside of a spar and over a
spreader to prevent the spar from bending. The traditional jib-boom
uses a martingale as shown which passes over a dolphin striker
to give it tension.

MAST BAND. Any band fitted around a mast from which stays, shrouds or
tackles are taken.

MAST CAP. A fitting over the top of the mast from which shrouds, stays and
halyards are taken.

MAST COAT. A canvas 'skirt' around the mast over the wedges where the
mast enters the vessel through the deck or cabin top. Sometimes called a
'skirt' or 'sock'.

MASTHEAD. The top of a mast.

MAST BAND

MAST CAP

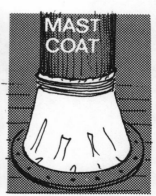

MAST COAT

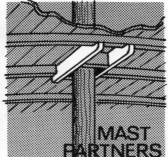

MASTHEAD LIGHT. A screened white light carried on the mainmast of engine propelled vessels. Optional on sailing craft.

MAST PARTNERS. 'Carlines' under the deck and between deck beams to give strength to the deck where the mast passes through.

MAST STEP. Traditionally the recess in the keelson where the mast stands. Now refers to any base on which the mast sits whether stepped on deck or into the keelson.

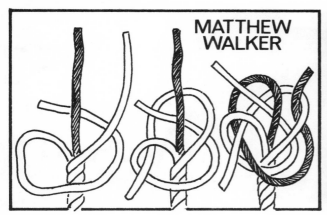

MATTHEW WALKER. A knot similar to the wall knot used to make a collar in the end of rope as shown.

MERCATOR CHART. A chart showing various areas of the world as straight lines by use of the method known as Mercator's Projection.
The illustration shows this in simple form. If a light were placed in the centre of a glass sphere, on the outside of which is a map of the world, the resultant projection onto a flat surface produces straight lines.
Mercator's Projection is limited by the distortion it experiences in high latitudes.

MERIDIAN. An imaginary line which passes north and south around the earth crossing the equator at right angles. *See* Longitude.

MERRIMAN CLIPS. A quick-action opening and closing 'shackle' used extensively in spinnaker work aboard small ships. It usually requires two hands to open or close and is thus not so fast as a snap-shackle. It is, however, much stronger.

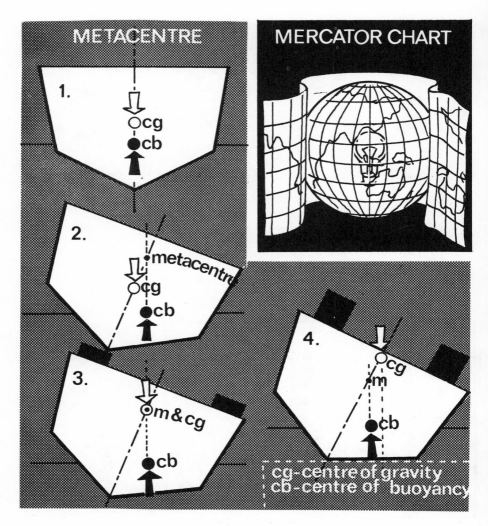

METACENTRE. The point above which the centre of gravity should never
    rise if a vessel is to remain stable. It is theoretically non-existent until the
    hull lists, at which time the centre of buoyancy moves outboard and a
    line drawn straight up from it will intersect the hull's centre line.
    The intersection point is the Metacentre. The illustration shows four
    situations in identical hulls. 1. The hull is at rest. The centre of gravity is
    the point where all downward forces are conceived to be centred. The
    centre of buoyancy is the point where the opposing forces of floatation
    are conceived to be centred. 2. When the hull is listed by any means
    the centre of gravity remains stationary whilst the centre of buoyancy
    moves towards the 'downhill' side. A vertical line drawn up through the
    centre of buoyancy will intersect the hull's centreline along which is
    established the centre of gravity. Where the two lines meet is the Metacentre.
    This hull is said to be in *stable equilibrium*. 3. When top weights are
    placed on the hull to raise the centre of gravity the hull is said to be in
    neutral equilibrium when the centre of gravity lies on the exact Metacentre.
    4. When the centre of gravity is raised above the Metacentre the hull is
    said to be in *unstable equilibrium* and there is a very real chance of
    it rolling right over.

164.

METAL THREAD

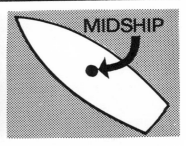

MIDSHIP

MIDDLE GROUND

METAL THREADS. The description of any bolt which is threaded along its entire length. Usually have either countersunk or round-head heads with a screwdriver slot. Are cheaper than normal bolts because less waste occurs when turned down from solid stock.

MICROBALLOONS. A synthetic (phenolic) filler for putties which gives the putty strength with minimum weight. Alternative synthetic fillers are 'Eccospheres' (glass) and polystyrene granules. Natural alternatives such as sawdust, pumice, vermiculite and diatomaceous earth are also successful when mixed into an epoxy or polyester putty base.

MICROMETER. Screw for making final adjustments when taking sextant sight. *See* Sextant *illustration.*

MIDDLE GROUND. Shoal area between two channels. If either end is buoyed or beaconed the object will be striped black and white or red and white, signifying that a vessel may pass to either side.

MIDSHIP. The approximate middle of the ship either fore and aft or transversely.

MIDSHIP FRAME. Sometimes called the 'main frame'. The largest section of a hull and the first one established by the designer and builder.

MIDSHIPMAN'S HITCH. A blackwall hitch with the loaded part of the rope taken over the hook once more.

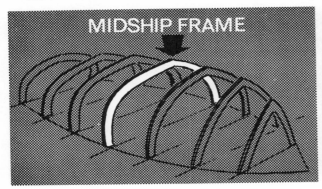

MIDSHIP FRAME

MIDSHIPMAN'S HITCH

MISSED STAYS. The failure of a vessel to go from one tack to another. When she turns into the wind but then falls off onto the same tack again. A common occurrence with shallow draught hulls with long keels.

MIZZEN. Fore and aft sail set on mizzen mast. Can be spelt mizen. *See* Ketch *illustration.*

MIZZEN MAST. The after mast on a ketch (*see* ketch) or the third mast from forward on vessels of three masts or more.

MODERATE VEE HULL. A hard chine hull of average deadrise. The angle tends to be about 15 degrees.

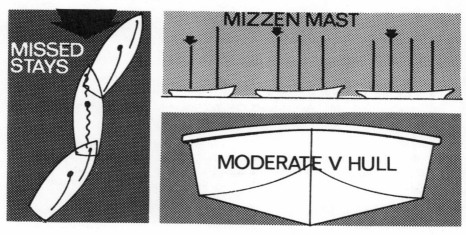

MONEL METAL. Used extensively for boat-nails and screws for small boat construction. Has the greatest resistance to deterioration of all the common alloys. Consists of 25 to 35% copper, 60 to 70% nickel, 1 to 4% iron and traces of manganese, silicon and carbon.

MONKEY'S FIST. A knot worked onto the end of a heaving rope to give it weight and make it carry. The knot is formed by making hanks of three turns each, as shown in the various stages illustratively.

MONKEY ISLAND. A screened navigation position above the bridge of a large ship.

MONOHULL. A single hull vessel. The word has experienced increasing use with the advent of multihulls.

MOONSAIL or MOONRAKER. A small extra sail set above the skysail on square rigged ships.

MOORING BUOY. A buoy anchored to the seabed by chain and weight, to which vessels may tie.

MORSE CODE. The alphabet and numbers represented by dots and dashes and transmitted by light or sound.

A • —	H • • • •	O — — —	V • • • —
B — • • •	I • •	P • — — •	W • — —
C — • — •	J • — — —	Q — — • —	X — • • —
D — • •	K — • —	R • — •	Y — • — —
E •	L • — • •	S • • •	Z — — • •
F • • — •	M — —	T —	
G — — •	N — •	U • • —	

1 • — — — —	6 — • • • •
2 • • — — —	7 — — • • •
3 • • • — —	8 — — — • •
4 • • • • —	9 — — — — •
5 • • • • •	0 — — — — —

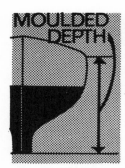

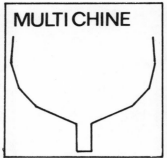

MORTICE BLOCK. A block that is chiselled from a solid piece of timber as against one that is 'built'.

MOTOR SAILER. A vessel equipped with engine and sails, each capable of driving her at near maximum hull speed. Usually designated in percentages. Thus a motor sailer equally capable under sail or engine is known as a 50/50. One which is under canvassed and thus enjoys better performance under engine than under sail might be called 60/40, etc.

MOULDED DEPTH. The distance between the keel and the top plank of the sides measured vertically.

MOULDED PLY. Term describing the construction method which uses narrow strips of ply glued in layers instead of timber when diagonally planked. *See* Cold Moulded.

MULE SAIL. An upside-down staysail hanked to a single backstay of a ketch. Sets above the mainsail and sheets to the mizen mast top. Collapses in following winds, otherwise an excellent addition.

MULTI CHINE. A hull with two or more chines on each side. A popular method with steel boats.

MULTI HULL. A general description of any vessel with two or more hulls. Typically, it refers to catamarans and trimarans.

MUNTZ METAL. An alloy containing approximately 60% copper and 40% tin. The word is often incorrectly used to describe an alloy of very poor quality. 'Muck' metal is correct here.

MUSHROOM ANCHOR. An umbrella shaped anchor ideal in mud and sand. Because it is almost impossible to lift out once dug in, it must be dropped with a trip-line as shown. Ideally, it should be used only as one of a group forming a permanent mooring.

MUSHROOM VENTILATOR. An opening vent ideal for use over hard to reach areas such as long counter sterns, etc. When open, ropes readily foul it and bend the threaded shaft.

1.

1. A stuffing box. This one is cast iron with white metal bushes to be used on a ferro-cement hull. The propellor shaft is supported by the stuffing box at one end and the stern bearing at the other end. Two stuffing boxes can be used. 2. The skeg on the Sydney flier, Leda is minimal but it is a skeg nonetheless. Its purpose is to support and protect the rudder. 3. A semi rotary pump makes an ideal in-line fuel pump. This one picks up fuel from below floor tanks and lifts it into the engine's gravity tank. Gate valves control and direct the flow. 4. Steel is very popular in small boat construction. Here we see the deck beams and cabin uprights being attached to a nearly completed hull. Note the minimal size of frames and stringers which give added space below decks in such vessels. 5. This is a balloon spinnaker. The word 'spinnaker' refers to any oversize headsail which sets flying. 6. The topsides of this vessel have what is known as 'tumble home'. That is, the sides turn in towards the deck and the maximum beam is below deck level. 7. A classic skylight.

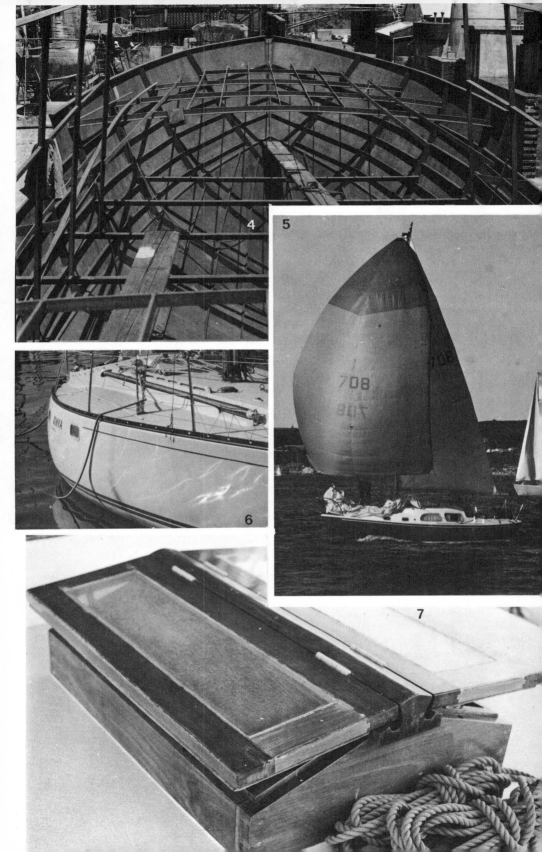

N

N. Flag of the International Code of Signals. Means 'No' ('negative' or 'the significance of the previous group should read in the negative'). Colour chequered blue and white.

NARROWS. Common name for the narrowest part of a waterway.

NAUTICAL MILE. One sea mile. 6080 feet which is 1/60 of a degree on the equator.

NAVEL PIPE. Pipe through which the anchor cable passes from the deck to its locker below.

NAVIGABLE. Said of an area safe for navigation.

NAVIGATION. The art of safely conducting a vessel from one place to another. There are two forms; coastal navigation and celestial navigation. The former requires only a knowledge of how to take compass bearings whilst the latter requires a knowledge of sextant work and the deduction of sight readings.

NAVIGATION LIGHTS. Those lights aboard ship to identify it and to indicate its position and course to other vessels. Basically this is achieved by the use of red and green side lights with white fore and aft lights all screened in such a way that only a certain combination can be seen at any one time. Light colours and their area of acceptable visibility are illustrated on page 174

NEAP TIDES. Those with less range than spring tides when the moon and sun are pulling more or less at right angles. Occur one week after full and new moon.

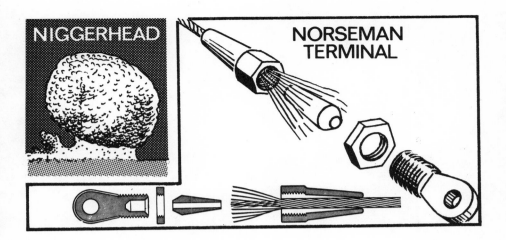

NEAPED. Said of a vessel which goes aground at spring high tide and the progressively lower tides of the neap period strands the vessel until spring tides once again reach her.

NEGRO HEAD BOLLARD. A single or twin pole bollard with an enlarged top.

NETT TONNAGE. The measurement of a vessel derived by deducting the space allowed for crew, engine room, etc., from the gross cubic capacity of the vessel. This ascertains the cargo carrying capacity and the result is tons in name only and not in fact.

NIGGERHEAD. Term sometimes used to describe a large isolated cluster of coral or a single large brain coral.

NOBLE METAL. A metal most able to resist deterioration due to electrolysis. For example, if a strip of aluminium and a strip of copper were tied together with wire and placed in sea water (which becomes the electrolyte) a weak electrical current will pass from one metal to the other destroying the least noble metal whilst the most noble metal survives. In this case the aluminium is least noble and will waste away ahead of the copper. Least noble metals are active and are *anodic*. Most noble metals are passive and are *cathodic*.

NORSEMAN TERMINAL. A swageless method of attaching rigging wire to a rigging screw. As shown, the wire is held by a cone which screws down hard on the wire ends.

NYLON ROPE. A synthetic of the polyamide family. In braided form is very popular as a sheet-rope owing to its limited stretch (only 7% under test), immense strength and excellent abrasion resistance. Tests show nylon will elongate up to 32% before breaking and is at least 2½ times stronger than equivalent good quality manila rope. It has a specific gravity of 1.14 and stands up well in sunlight although excessive exposure will downgrade it.

NAVIGATION LIGHTS

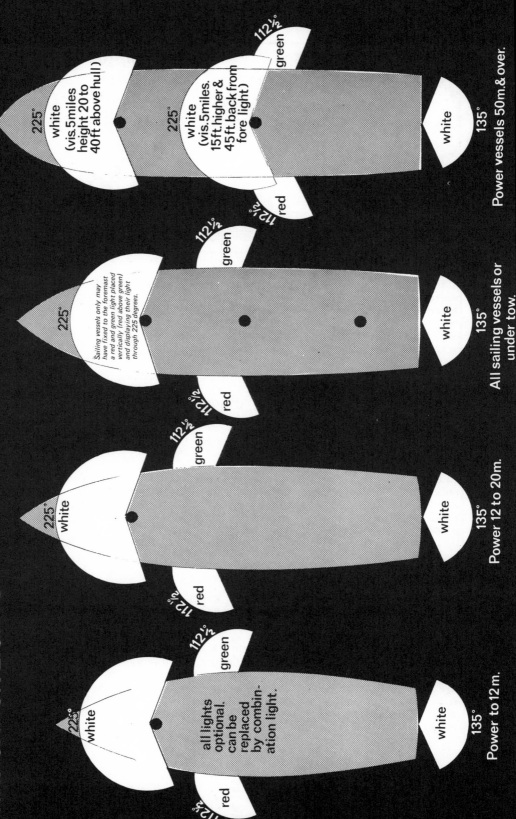

Power vessels 50m. & over.

- white (vis.5miles height 20 to 40ft above hull) — 225°
- white (vis.5miles. 15ft.higher & 45 ft.back from fore light) — 225°
- green — 112½°
- red — 112½°
- white — 135°

All sailing vessels or under tow.

- 225° — Sailing vessels only may have fixed to the foremast a red and green light placed vertically (red above green) and displaying their light through 225 degrees.
- green — 112½°
- red — 112½°
- white — 135°

Power 12 to 20m.

- white — 225°
- green — 112½°
- red — 112½°
- white — 135°

Power to 12 m.

- white — 225°
- green — 112½°
- red — 112½°
- white — 135°
- all lights optional. can be replaced by combination light.

Modern Racing Yacht

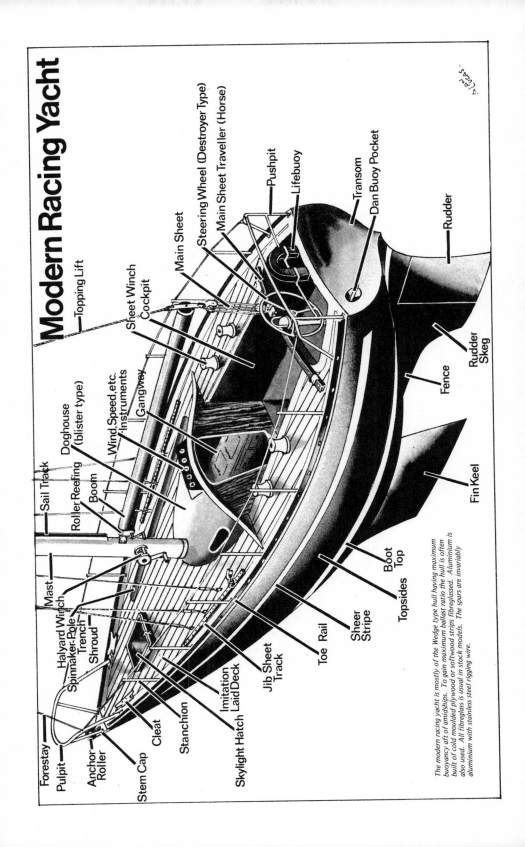

Topping Lift
Sail Track
Doghouse (blister type)
Roller Reefing
Boom
Wind Speed etc. Instruments
Gangway
Sheet Winch
Cockpit
Main Sheet
Steering Wheel (Destroyer Type)
Main Sheet Traveller (Horse)
Pushpit
Lifebuoy
Transom
Dan Buoy Pocket
Rudder

Forestay
Pulpit
Anchor Roller
Stem Cap
Mast
Halyard Winch
Spinnaker Pole Trench
Shroud
Cleat
Stanchion
Imitation Laid Deck
Skylight Hatch
Jib Sheet Track
Toe Rail
Sheer Stripe
Boot Top
Topsides
Fin Keel
Fence
Rudder Skeg

The modern racing yacht is mostly of the Wedge type hull having maximum buoyancy aft of amidships. To gain maximum ballast ratio the hull is often built of cold moulded plywood or softwood strips fibreglassed. Aluminium is also used. All fibreglass is usual in stock models. The spars are invariably aluminium with stainless steel rigging wire.

Traditional Yacht Construction

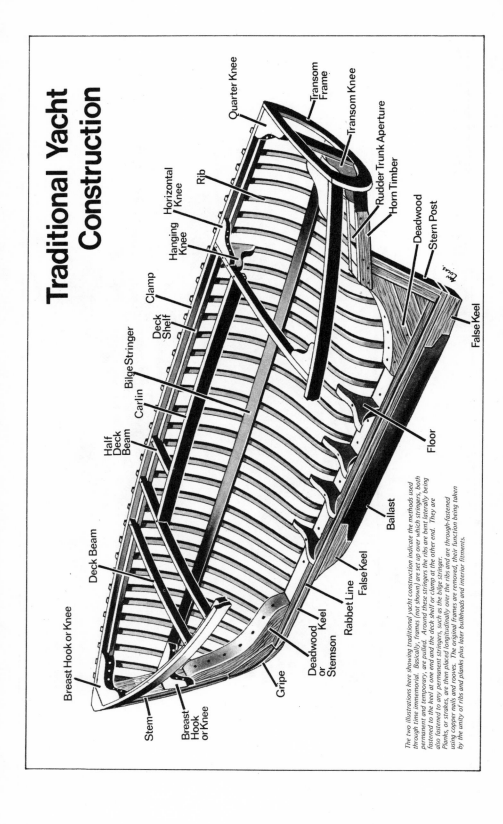

The two illustrations here showing traditional yacht construction indicate the methods used through time immemorial. Basically, frames (not shown) are set up over which stringers, both permanent and temporary, are pulled. Around these stringers the ribs are bent laterally being fastened to the keel at one end and the deck shelf or clamp at the other end. They are also fastened to any permanent stringers, such as the bilge stringer.
Planks, or strakes, are then placed longitudinally over the ribs and are through-fastened using copper nails and rooves. The original frames are removed, their function being taken by the unity of ribs and planks plus later bulkheads and interior fitments.

Quarter Knee

Transom Frame

Transom Knee

Rudder Trunk Aperture

Horn Timber

Deadwood

Stern Post

Rib

Horizontal Knee

Hanging Knee

Clamp

Deck Shelf

Bilge Stringer

Carlin

Half Deck Beam

Deck Beam

Breast Hook or Knee

Stem

Breast Hook or Knee

Gripe

Deadwood or Stemson

Rabbet Line

False Keel

Ballast

Floor

False Keel

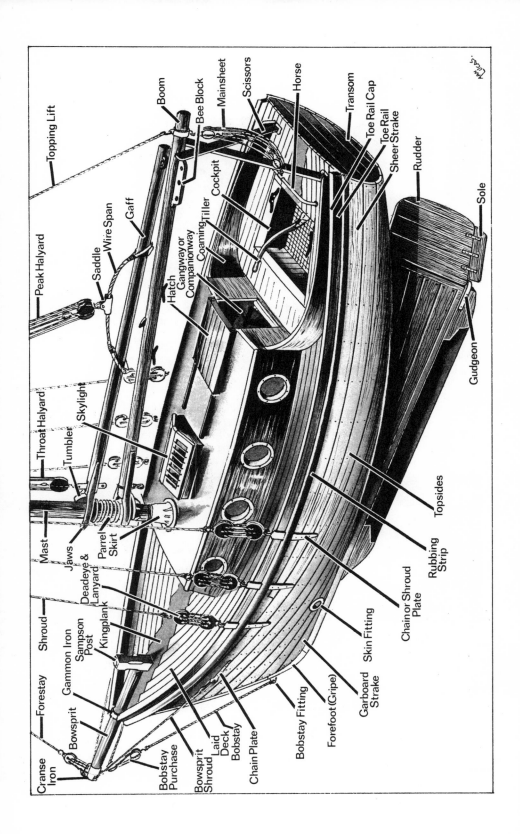

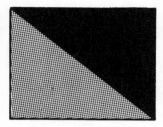

O. Flag of the International Code of Signals meaning; 'man overboard'. It is diagonally divided into two areas of red and yellow.

OAKUM. Rope that has been unlaid and teased out for the purpose of caulking a seam. It is usually tarred to make it more controllable and long lasting.

OAR. Device used for rowing a boat consisting of a blade at one end and a loom at the other.

OAR LOCK. *See* Rowlock.

OAR STOP. The collar between the loom and shaft of an oar to prevent it sliding out of the rowlock. Originally made of leather or copper and leather. Now commonly a one piece moulding of plastic. Leather stops are preferable because of their greater friction with the rowlock.

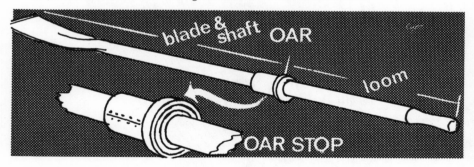

OCCULTING. Said of a light which is visible for longer periods than it is invisible. It is the opposite to flashing, which has longer periods of dark than light.

OCEAN. Describes the expanse of water covering the globe. There are only five oceans, viz; the Pacific, Atlantic, Indian, Arctic and Antarctic. These are further broken up into 'seas'. For example, the south-west corner of the Pacific Ocean, between Australia and New Zealand is called the Tasman Sea.

OFF AND ON. The progress along a coastline when it is alternatively brought up close then stood off.

OFFING. The area of sea that lies between the horizon and a point half way between the horizon and the observer. To 'make an offing' is to get a safe distance offshore.

OFF THE WIND. Sailing with the wind abaft the beam. Can also be said of a vessel not sailing as close to the wind as she could whilst close hauled.

OHM. Unit of electrical resistance. The force of one ampere of current at a pressure of one volt equals one ohm.

OIL BAG. Any soft container that is filled with oil which continually spills from it via a small hole. This tends to prevent seas breaking when streamed out from a vessel during bad weather. Its use is questionable in practical conditions because of the potential mess in getting it ready then streaming it.

OILSKINS. A word still occasionally used to describe any apparel designed for use aboard ship during rainy or bad weather. Derived from the fact that the original waterproof clothing was made of calico treated with linseed oil.

OIL TANKER. A ship fitted with tanks used to carry various grades of fuel and oil. Vessels of this type have been built to gigantic proportions exceeding 500,000 tons.

OLD MAN. Typical nickname for the captain of any ship.

OMBROMETER. Rain gauge.

ONE DESIGN CLASS. Boats of identical design which do not race to a handicap.

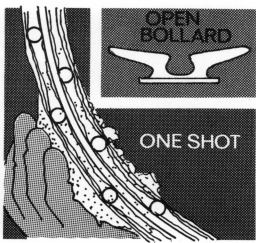

ONE SHOT METHOD. In ferro-cement boat building where the plaster is applied to the armature of mesh and rods in 'one shot'. It is pushed through the armature to the other side and thus fills in one application as against two. *See* Two Shot Method.

OPEN BOLLARD. Name sometimes given to a cleat which can also be used as a fairlead.

OPEN FRAME R'SCREW

OPEN HAWSE

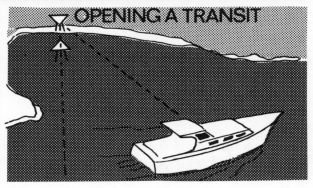

OPENING A TRANSIT

OPEN FRAME RIGGING SCREW. As shown, a type of rigging tensioner which consists of right and left hand threaded ends which screw into an open frame. It tends to be the weakest type and as such is not recommended on boats.

OPEN HAWSE. Said of cables leading directly to their anchors when two are laid, one from each side of the bow.

OPENING A TRANSIT. Moving off a transit line. For example, when a vessel passes across two channel leading beacons she is said to be 'opening a transit.'

ORLOP DECK. The lowest deck in a battleship.

OSSEL KNOT AND HITCH. Used in net making when it hangs from a backing rope by its headrope. The lines by which it hangs are known as 'ossels.'

OTTER BOARDS. Boards rigged in such a way that when towed they sheer out, away from each other. A net strung between the two is thus kept open as it drags along the bottom of the sea. Used in all forms of trawling. Usually built from hardwood framed with steel.

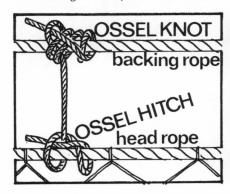

OSSEL KNOT
backing rope
OSSEL HITCH
head rope

OTTER BOARD

OUTBOARD MOTOR. A self-contained petrol driven unit which clamps to the stern of a boat. Originally of low horse-power designed for small boats, now available in a power range reaching 280 horse-power and used for high speed racing, skiing, etc.

OUTBOARD WELL. The 'cockpit' sometimes incorporated into the stern of a boat designed to carry an outboard. It permits a low transom yet prohibits the introduction of water into the bilge.

OUTER JIB. The one in front of the inner jib.

OUTFOOT. To out sail another boat. Usually refers to the situation when both boats are sailing — or 'footing', to windward.

OUTHAUL. Any line used to haul a sail or spar out beyond the limit of human reach. Typically, the flying jib is outhauled along the jib boom.

OUTPOINT. To sail a fraction closer to the wind than another boat.

OUTRIGGER. The framework extending outside a rowing boat to support the rowlocks. Typically a racing skiff. 2. The apparatus used to support a small 'hull' to prevent the main hull from capsizing.

OVERFALL. The water rushing off a shoal area by the action of tide or current and 'falling' into deeper water. The resultant disturbance on the surface in the form of 'boiling' waves is known as an overfall.

OVERHAND KNOT. The simplest knot of all as shown.

OVERHANGS. That part of a vessel which projects beyond the waterline either fore or aft.

OVERHAUL. To extend the distance between two blocks by running off the tackles. 2. To repair and maintain any machinery, hull or rigging. 3. To overtake another vessel.

OVERLAP. When the bow of an overtaking vessel projects beyond the stern of the overtaken vessel.

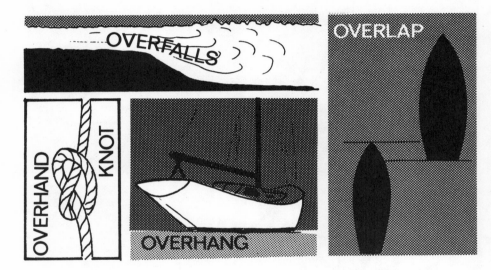

P

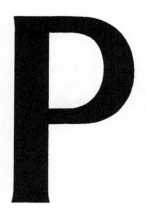

P. Flag of the International Code of Signals meaning; 'All persons should report aboard as the vessel is about to proceed to sea.' At sea it may be used by fishing vessels to mean; 'my nets have come fast upon an obstruction.' Known as the 'Blue Peter'. Coloured blue with white oblong in centre.

PACKET. Loosely applies to any vessel, but specifically refers to one employed on a regular run carrying mail, passengers and cargo.

PAD. The shaped timber fixed above a deck beam to give it camber.

PADDLE. A small oar used to propel small craft — especially canoes, which is gripped in both hands.

PADDLE WHEEL. The framework which carries the paddle boards on a ship propelled by paddle wheels.

PADDY'S PURCHASE. A derogative term applying to tackles whose power is negligible and useless.

PAD

PADDLE WHEEL

PADDLE

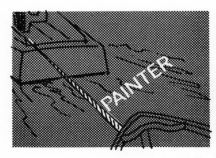
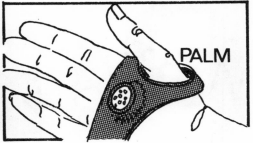

PAINTER. A rope secured to the bow of a small boat used for towing or making fast.

PALM. A leather hand band with a steel disc for pushing a sailmaker's needle when sewing. 2. The part of an Admiralty pattern or fisherman's anchor which provides a holding surface. *See* Admiralty Pattern Anchor.

PANTING. The stress action on a hull caused by water pressure outside. Typically the bow area 'pants' when pitching into a headsea. It is prevented by the addition of a 'panting beam' across the bow.

PANTRY PUMP. Any pump used for lifting either fresh or salt water to the galley. Sometimes called a 'galley pump.'

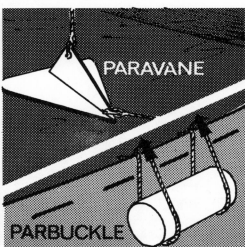

PARALLEL RULER. Two rulers connected by steel or plastic beams which can be 'walked' across a chart to transfer a line from one area to another.

PARAVANE. As shown, a device towed on both sides of a vessel to reduce rolling in a seaway. Popular on trawlers. Originally used as a mine clearing device.

PARBUCKLE. A method of hauling aboard, or up an incline, any round object such as a barrel or spar. The object itself acts as a 'pulley.'

PARCEL. To wrap a wire in material such as canvas or hessian prior to serving with marlin or similar. Parcelling is always done *with* the lay and can be greased or treated in some way to further protect the host.

Handle

Gland

Gland Packing

Cap

Stem

The Pantry Pump is traditionally made of brass, either polished or chromed. There are alternative types available built of plastic. Although working on the same basic principle their components are often impossible to get at for maintenance. As a result they must be scrapped after the smallest breakdown.

Outlet

The basic action of the Pantry Pump is shown below. On the up stroke (left) the ball valve within the cage at the bottom of the stem closes, the suction it creates opening the ball valve at the bottom of the pump body. Any water above the closed valve escapes through the outlet. On the down stroke (right) the bottom valve closes and the top valve opens forcing water from the bottom of the pump body into the top of same.

Body

Ball Valve

Valve Cage

Leather Washer

Nut

Ball Valve

Inlet & Valve Housing

Pantry Pump

PARREL. Circular rope used to hold a gaff sail against the mast.

PARREL TRUCKS. Wooden or plastic balls threaded onto the parrel to prevent it griping against the mast.

PARTNERS. Short fore and aft timbers fastened to the underside of a deck to spread the load and strengthen the area where a mast, capstan, etc., pierces the deck. *See* Mast Partners.

PATENT LOG. A device streamed astern to ascertain speed and distance. *See* Log.

PAWL. A pivoted bar resting upon a toothed rack to prevent opposite movement. Common method of preventing a capstan or chain gypsy from running away whilst being worked. The devil's claw is a type of pawl which acts directly on the chain itself. *See* Devil's Claw.

PAY. To run pitch or synthetic compound into the seam between two planks.

PAY OFF. To discharge the crew. 2. Said of the vessel's bow when moving away from the wind.

PAY OUT. To run out a cable in a controlled manner.

PEA. The extreme end of an anchor's palm. *See* Admiralty Pattern Anchor *illustration.*

PEAK. The upper corner of a gaff sail.

PEAK HALYARD. Rope used to hoist the peak of a gaff.

PEAK TANKS. Tanks placed in the extreme ends of a hull and filled with water to trim the vessel.

PELICAN HOOK. A hinged hook which is held by a sliding collar. Can be released quickly. Ideal for removable stays, trailer winch cable attachment, etc.

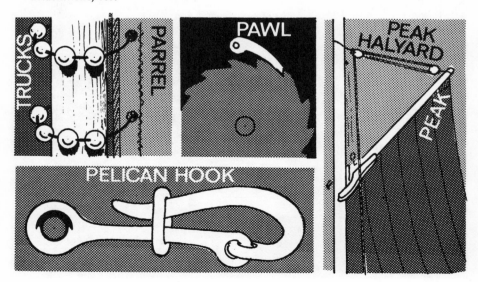

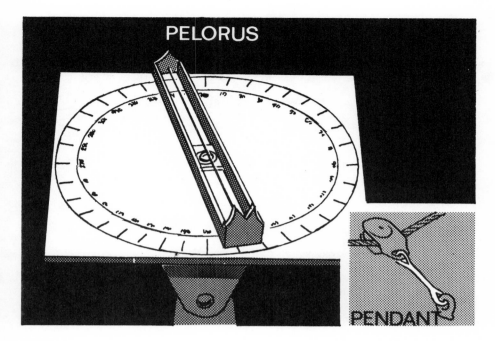

PELORUS

PENDANT

PELORUS. A dumb compass dial, or protractor, over which is fitted a fully pivoting arm along which sights are taken in navigation. Ideally suited where sights cannot be taken across a compass. The pelorus sight is taken and read at the exact same time a compass reading is taken. To arrive at the correct bearing the two bearings are added. Thus if the pelorus reads 210 degrees whilst the compass reads 95 degrees, the actual bearing would be 305 degrees. If the total exceeds 360 degrees, 360 is subtracted to find the correct bearing. The name 'pelorus' is also given to the pivoting bar only where it fits over the top of a compass and thus gives direct readings.

PENDANT. A length of cable connecting a block to a fixed part of the vessel.

PENNANT. A four sided flag with a head deeper than the fly. Sometimes spelt 'pendant.'

PERIGEE. That point in the orbital path of a heavenly body where it comes closest to earth. The point farthest away is called the 'apogee.'

PIER. Wharf, jetty.

PILE DRIVING. Said of a vessel when lifting her forefoot out of the water then plunging down into the next wave. Most violent when the hull is of a length shorter than the distance between two waves.

PILES. Concrete or timber supports to a pier, etc.

PILOT. A person of deep sea qualifications employed by a local authority to take a ship into or out of port or along restricted coasts where the captain requires local knowledge. A pilot is mandatory in most harbours until the captain has entered harbour enough times to enjoy a 'pilot exemption.'

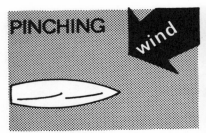

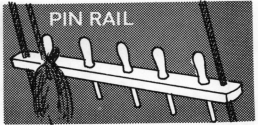

PILOT BOAT. The vessel used to carry the pilot from shore to ship. It operates from a 'pilot station.'

PILOT WATERS. Any area where the service of a pilot is compulsory.

PINCHING. Sailing too close to the wind to be efficient.

PINNACE. A tender to larger vessels of the Royal Navy.

PIN RAIL. A horizontal rail, usually fixed to the shrouds, with belaying pins standing vertically in holes.

PINTLE. A fitting by which the rudder hangs. *See* Gudgeon *illustration.*

PIPE DECK PLATES. Another name for 'Deck filler.' *See* Filler Cap *illustration.*

PIPE FRAMES. Frames made of ordinary water or steam pipe especially in the construction of ferro-cement boats. The old method called for their inclusion into the finished structure but recent development tends to use the pipe frames as a jig only which is ripped out and thrown away after plastering leaving the hull frameless or with web frames only.

PITCH. Used for paying decks. Is a distillation of tar.

PITCH OF PROPELLOR. Distance vessel would advance with one turn of the propellor if there were no slip. The pitch is stated as this distance. Thus, a 20 inch by 18 inch propellor would have a diameter of 20 inches and a theoretical distance travelled in one revolution of 18 inches.

PITCHING. The motion of a vessel when plunging into a headsea.

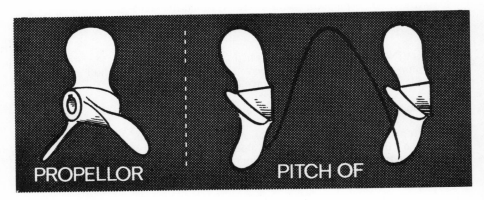

PITCH OF RIVETS

PITCHING

PITCH POLE

PLANK ON EDGE

PLANKING CLAMP

PLIMSOLL MARK

PITCH OF RIVETS. Distance between rivets measured from centre to centre.

PITCH POLE. The act of end-over-ending where the vessel goes through 360 degrees stern over bow.

PLANK. Part of the cladding on the hull and deck. Mostly called a 'strake' when on the hull. *See* Strake.

PLANK ON EDGE. Name given to deep and narrow yachts. Invariably they have excessive ballast and are also called 'lead mines'. The hull of such types tends to be beautifully balanced and vice free.

PLANKING CLAMP. A simple tool used to hold a plank against the rib until fastened.

PLASTIC BOATS. General term used to describe any boat built of resin and fibreglass.

PLEDGE. A length of oakum prepared for caulking.

PLIMSOLL LINE OR MARK. A load-line marking on the side of a ship showing the safe limit to which cargo may be loaded under varying conditions. The name came from the markings on British ships owned by Sir Samuel Plimsoll whose efforts to prevent dangerous overloading eventually became law under an Act of Parliament.

PLOUGH ANCHOR. An identical type to the C.Q.R. anchor.

PLUG. Alternative name for the male mould of a boat hull. Commonly used for the amateur building of foam-sandwich and fibreglass hulls and the production-line building of ferro-cement hulls. The plug is always made of timber, usually of battens close together.

PLUMMER BLOCK. A shaft bearing which is either roller or friction type whose housing bolts to a horizontal surface.

PLYWOOD. Two or more laminates of thin timber veneer, the grains of which lie at right angles to each other to give uniform strength in all directions. There are many varieties from which to choose and the boat builder is not always restricted to the expensive marine grades. Many of the construction, flooring, crate and concrete formwork plywoods are glued with top grade waterproof ply equal to any marine grade glue. When waterproof glue is used it is called an 'A Grade Bond'.
The greatest difference in quality of the A Grade bonded plywoods lies in the type of timber in the veneers and the care with which it has been assembled. Marine grade must have only the best timbers and they must be assembled without voids. Construction plys, etc., use cheaper timber and voids are permissible up to a certain limit. Only marine grade ply should be used in hull construction, but one of the A Grade bonded alternatives can be used in interior fitments.

POINT. A reef point. 2. A point of a compass is 1/32 of 360 degrees which is 11¼ degrees. 3. Said of a vessel when sailing to windward. She is 'pointing' high or low depending on her windward qualities.

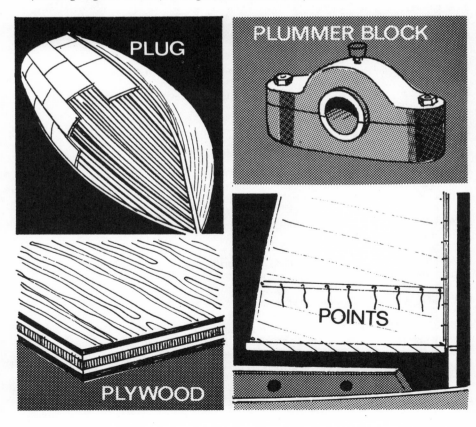

PLUG

PLUMMER BLOCK

PLYWOOD

POINTS

POLYAMIDE. This is the family name for nylon which is used in many
facets of boat building and rigging. Commonly used in bearing surfaces,
the moulding of small fittings, sheaves and rope. Nylon was the first
of the truly synthetic fibres, the discovery of which is accredited to
Wallace Carothers and first introduced in 1939 by Du Pont.
See Nylon Rope.

POLYESTER. A resin used most commonly in glass fibre construction, it
being easier to use, faster to set and more readily sanded than other resins.
It is also the cheapest type and is thus the only one economically possible
for the manufacturer. Polyester fibres, when made into cloth under such
well known trade names as Dacron and Terylene, are extruded from a
chemical solution made up of dihydric alcohol and terepthalic acid.
Polyester rope is known as Dacron or Terylene. *See* Terylene Rope.

POLYETHYLENE. The family name for 'silver rope'. *See* Silver Rope
for details.

POLYPROPYLENE. Derived from the polyolefin family, polypropylene is
commonly used for rope making. It enjoys the following properties.
Floats in water, will recover by 95 percent after being stretched 10 percent,
has excellent abrasion resistance because of its waxiness and its moisture
regain after being underwater is nil.

POLYURETHANE. The urethanes are a fairly recent development, their
most outstanding character being that they can be made thermosetting
or thermoplastic. Polyurethane is a popular, hard wearing paint ideal for
application onto other resins such as the painting of a fibreglass boat, etc.

POLYVINYL ALCOHOL. Family name for the rope known as 'Vinylon'
which replaced the name 'Kuralon'. *See* Kuralon Rope. Polyvinyl resin
has properties somewhere between the polyesters and epoxies but is less
stable whilst working and is not recommended to the amateur.

PONTOON. Any craft used for supporting weights by its own buoyancy
without actually transporting them. Commonly used in marina
construction and for pontoon 'wharves'. Originally built of coppered
timber, now in ferro-cement.

POOP. The raised deck aft.

POOPED. Said of a vessel when seas break aboard over the stern whilst
running with the wind.

191.

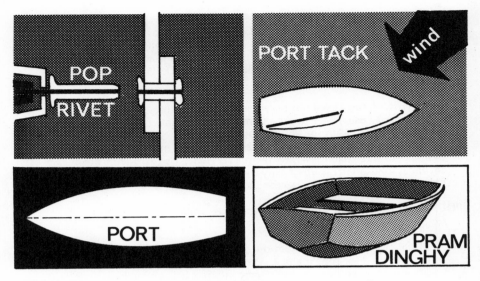

POP RIVETS. A method of fastening metal plates together or to frames where there is no access behind for threading a nut or the holding of a normal riveting dolly. As shown, the rivet is pushed through, expanded and cut in the one operation using the correct gun.

PORT. The left hand side of any vessel looking forward. Only boats can have a port or starboard side and this must be born in mind to avoid confusion when advised to pass a navigational object to port or starboard. 2. Any opening in the hull's sides to admit air or light or to disperse water from the deck.

PORT HOLE. An opening in the ship's side through which air and light can pass. *See* Deadlight *illustration.*

PORT TACK. Sailing with the wind blowing in over the port side.

PRAM DINGHY. A small tender with a cut-off bow, or 'pram' bow.

PRATIQUE. Being granted permission to land in a foreign port after a vessel is checked by local medical officers. The 'Q' flag is flown when requesting pratique.

PRICKER. Thin marlin spike used to prick holes into material preparatory to sewing and for opening small diameter rope when splicing.

PROLONGED BLAST. Sounding a siren, whistle or horn for a period of 4 to 6 seconds.

PROPELLOR. A multi bladed 'fan' used to propel a vessel. The two bladed type is ideal for yachts where the blade can be 'hidden' behind the stern timber when not in use where it offers the least resistance. In large cruisers, trawlers and motor-sailers the four bladed propellor is considered as being the best because of its superior balance. *For further information see* Pitch of Propellor.

PROPELLOR SHAFT. The power transmission shaft between the engine and the propellor.

192.

PROPELLOR TUBE. The case sealed inside the actual hull material with bearings at each end which support the propellor shaft. This tube can be either oil or grease filled depending on the method used which further prevents water from entering the hull.

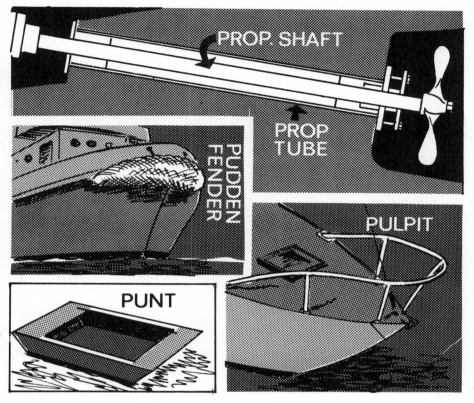

PUDDEN FENDER. A thick fender fitted around the bow. Typically on tugs. Originally filled with 'puddening' which is rope strands.

PULLEY CLIP. Alternative name for 'bridge eye'. If fitted with a bush it can be called 'bulls eye fairlead'. *See illustrations under those headings.*

PULPIT. A crew guard rail embracing the bow or stern of a vessel.

PUMP. Any device designed to lift a fluid and discharge it into another container or over the side. The various types used on boats are illustrated in exploded view and will be found on page 78 132, 185 and 220.

PUMP WELL. A special well into which the strum box fits and from where the dregs of the liquid being pumped gravitate towards. *See* Strum Box.

PUNCHINGS. Pellets of steel from the manufacture of any item where holes are punched. Because of their maximum concentration of weight they make popular ballast mixed with cement and poured into the keels of steel, fibreglass and ferro-cement hulls.

PUNT. Small craft designed to float in shallow water and propelled by a pole which rests on the bottom of the waterway.

PURCHASE. The amount of 'leverage' gained in blocks and tackle. Stated as a unit of advantage. For example, a tackle consisting of two double blocks, as illustrated, enjoys a mechanical advantage of 4 to 1. The advantage can be ascertained by counting the number of moving parts of the rope and the number of non moving parts (standing part).´

PUSHPIT. Name sometimes given to the stern pulpit. In fact the name has become so well accepted that most people think of a pulpit as being a bow structure only.

PUT ABOUT. Another way of saying going about. From one tack to the other.

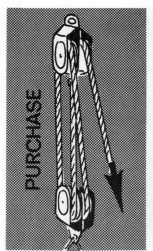
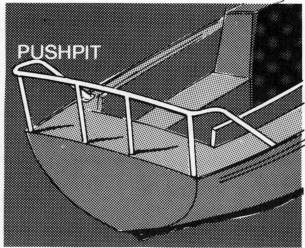

The two yachts shown opposite have a hull of the 'symmetrical' (top) and 'wedge' (bottom) type. The symmetrical type is a balanced hull having maximum buoyancy amidships. It has few vices on any point of sailing but, conversely, it does not enjoy extremes of performance. The wedge type has maximum buoyancy aft of amidships with consequently fine bow sections. As a result they can be difficult to keep under control running hard off a wind but enjoy maximum efficiency when beating upwind.

The sextant shown in the bottom left hand corner is the 'micrometer' type. Seconds are read off a revolving drum (the micrometer) after it has been used to gain final, exact adjustment. This type is shown in exploded view opposite its description.

The stern tube shown here is fitted to a steel hull. Normally, a stern bearing is placed outside and a stuffing box is placed inside the hull. The propellor shaft is supported by these two fittings and grease is pumped into the tube to give a final seal from the sea outside.

194.

1.

2.

1. The classic wooden steering wheel is found
only on traditional vessels nowadays.
The spokes were always a danger. 2. A three
masted topsail schooner. 3. An interesting
method of stowing spinnaker poles. 4. This
beautiful stern is a 'transom' stern. 5. A tiller
extension is clearly visible in the skipper's hand.
6. A typical trawler. The gallows behind the
wheelhouse carry the Otter Boards and
trailing gear.

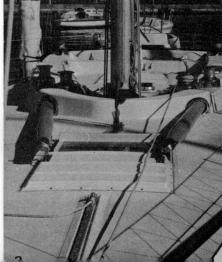

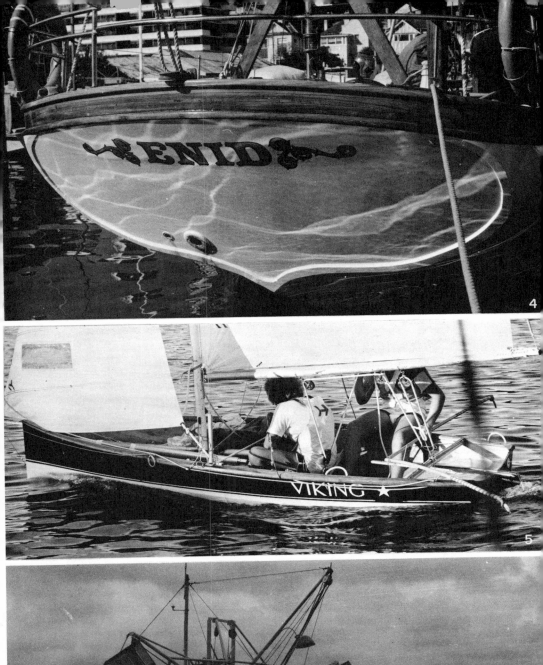

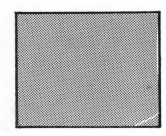

Q. Flag of the International Code of Signals meaning; 'My vessel is healthy and I request pratique'. Coloured plain yellow.

QUADRANT. Quarter of a circle. A navigational instrument now replaced by the sextant. 2. The fitting over the top of a rudder stock where steering is effected by ropes or chain.

QUADRANT THROTTLE. A control lever which holds its position by the friction of a serrated edge along the quadrant.

QUARTER. The stern 'corners' of a vessel. Anywhere from aft of the beam to one side of the centre-line.

QUARTER BLOCK. The block attached to the yard through which the clewline is rove.

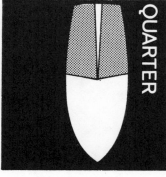
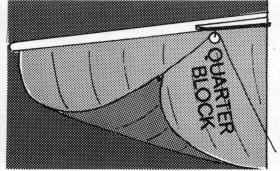

QUARTER DECK. From the mainmast to right aft. Where a vessel has poop deck it ends at the poop break.

QUARTERING. Sailing with the wind over the quarter. A 'quartering wind'.

QUARTER KNEES. A lateral knee or 'hook' joining the deck shelf or clamp to the transom.

QUAY. Another name for wharf, jetty or pier but more generally accepted as meaning a commercial area.

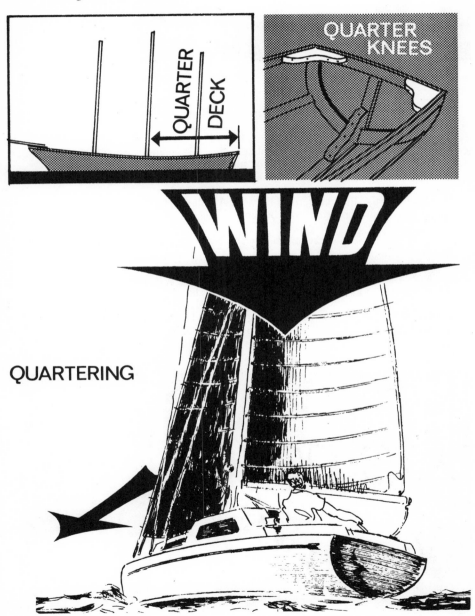

QUARTER DECK

QUARTER KNEES

WIND

QUARTERING

R. Flag of the International Code of Signals meaning; 'I have received your last signal'. A red background with a yellow cross.

RABBET. A recess along a piece of timber to give a snug and flush landing to a mating piece. Typically, the stem and keel of a timber hull is rabbeted to receive the strakes as shown.

RACE. A strong localised current in the sea. Also a shortening of the term 'ball race' which is a type of shaft bearing.

RACK BLOCK. A multi sheave block used to lead running rigging from one direction to another.

RACKING. The action of two structural members trying to work independently of each other despite restraining devices.

RACKING SEIZING. As shown, a seizing designed to dampen the racking moment between the standing part of a cable or rope and the tail. It is put on in a series of figure-of-eights then served down.

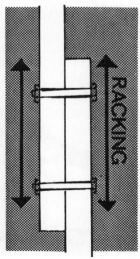

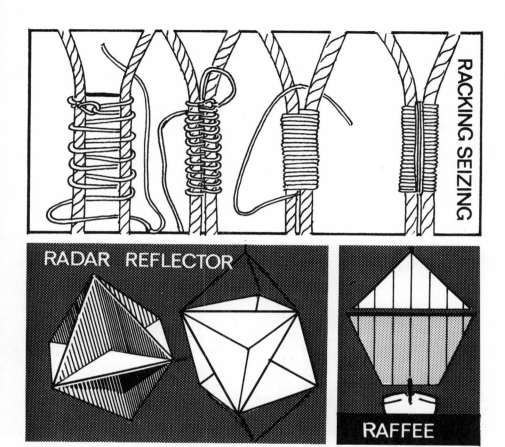

RADAR REFLECTOR

RAFFEE

RADAR REFLECTOR. A beacon situated on a reef or other navigational hazard designed to give maximum display on a ship's radar screen.
2. A diamond shape device fixed to the rigging of a small boat to give it maximum display. It should be fixed as shown, the angle of the metal surfaces in relation to the horizontal plane being important for maximum reflection.

RADIO DIRECTION FINDER. An electronic device capable of receiving most medium and short range radio signals then indicating the relevant bearing on which it is received. This is achieved by the fact that an aerial is directional. If turned in a full circle it will increase or decrease the radio signal's strength.

RAFFEE. A triangular sail set above the highest yard on a square-rigged vessel.

RAG BOLT. Essentially a 'dump' with jagged cuts across the shank to prevent it working out once driven into timber.

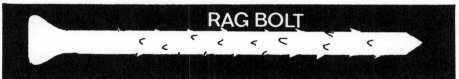

RAG BOLT

RAIL. The bulwark capping. It is known as the 'main rail'. If another rail is situated above the main rail it is called the 'topgallant rail'.

RAISED HEAD SCREW. An ordinary wood screw having a head designed to remain above the surface. Ideal where removal is necessary.

RAKE. The angle of an object which inclines from the vertical position. Examples; raked bow or raked funnels.

RAM BOW. A bow having its forefoot further forward than the stemhead. Raked backwards. Named after fighting ships of old which had ramming devices fitted at or below the waterline projecting from the bow.

RANGE OF TIDE. The difference between the height of low water and the height of high water of the same day. Thus a low tide of 0.4 metres to a high tide of 4.2 metres has a range of 3.8 metres.

RATCATCHER. A metal shield placed on a berthing hawser to prevent rats climbing aboard.

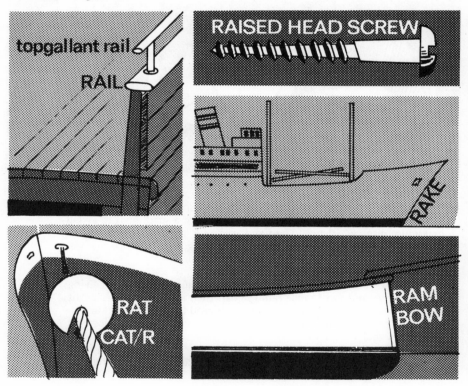

RATCHET BLOCK. A block whose sheave is controlled by a ratchet to prevent it turning in the opposite direction.

RATING RULE. In racing. An alternative to physical handicapping of sailing boats which permits them to start a race at the same time. It is a collection of measurements, etc. which, when computed to a simple figure, shows what could be expected of the vessel over a certain distance. At the end of the race her time is corrected to show the handicap result.

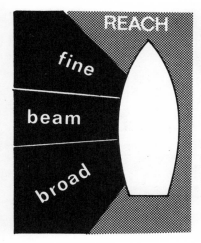

RATLINES. Ropes lashed across the shrouds to provide a footing and
handhold for crew going aloft. The best substitute is wooden or metal
rungs which are less dangerous and more comfortable than rope.
A method of fastening 'wooden ratlines' is shown.

REACH. Sailing with the wind somewhere over the beam. If forward of the
beam it is called a 'fine reach', on the beam a 'beam reach' and abaft
the beam a 'broad reach'. When the wind is right angles to the course
it can be called a 'soldier's wind'.

REACHING. Sailing with the wind on the beam or forward of it. Tacking
to windward.

RED LEAD. Basically a mixture of lead oxide (PB_3O_4) and linseed oil.
One of the original and still the best primers for timber and steel.

REEF. To shorten sail by reducing its area by a variety of methods.
See Jiffy Reefing, Roller Reefing and Roller Furling. 2. A coral or rock
underwater rampart.

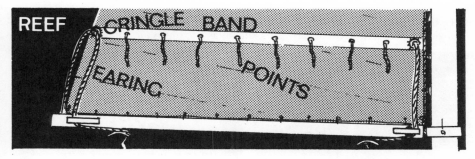

REEF BAND. A strengthening strip of material sewn across the sail where
the reef points hang.

REEF CRINGLE. Thimble in leech of sail in line with the reef points to
take reef earing.

REEF EARING. Short length of rope (pendant) for hauling down and
securing the reef cringle.

203.

REEF KNOT. A simple knot, tied as shown.

REEF POINTS. Short lengths of line attached to the reef band of a sail.
They hang through the sail on both sides and are tied under the boom
when the sail is reefed.

REEF TACKLE. Small block and tackles used to exert more weight when
hauling down the reef cringle.

REEVE. To pass a rope through any opening be it block, cringle or eye.

REFRACTION. The bending of a light or heat ray as it passes from one
medium to another medium of different density. A typical example
of this is when the sun is low on the horizon and is therefore penetrating
maximum thickness of atmosphere between it and the observer.
As a result it always appears higher than it is. Refraction decreases
as the sun climbs.

RESORCINAL FORMALDEHYDE RESIN. A wood glue of high water
resistance consisting of a brown honey-like liquid to which a powder
hardener is mixed. This glue is most ideal for laminating and is used in
the manufacture of plywood where an 'A Grade' bond is demanded.

RHUMB. A line on the earth's surface that cuts all meridians at a constant
angle other than at right angles. It is known as a loxodromic curve.

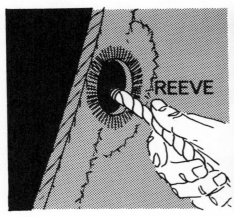

RIB. Transverse structural members of a wooden vessel.

RIBBAND CARVEL. A method of building where fore and aft battens are placed beneath every seam of the strakes. It has the advantage of preventing the caulking from driving through and upsetting the integrity of the seam. *See* Batten Carvel.

RIDGE ROPE. Rope or wire over which an awning is spread.

RIDING BITTS. *See* Bitts.

RIDING LIGHT. An all round white light hoisted forward when at anchor. Vessels of more than 150 feet in length must display a second white light from the stern which must be no less than 15 feet lower than the forward light.

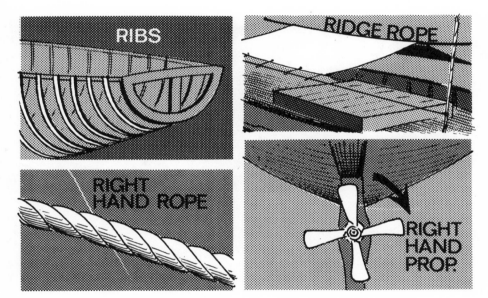

RIG. The way in which a vessel is fitted with masts and spars. Ketch Rig, Schooner Rig, etc. 2. To rig a vessel is to fit her out with masts and spars.

RIGGER. One who rigs a vessel or any shorebound installation requiring wire support, lifting gear, etc.

RIGGING. All the paraphernalia required to equip a vessel ready to sail. Divided into two main groups known as 'running rigging' and 'standing rigging'. Running rigging describes that which actually moves such as sheets and halyards. Standing rigging describes the non moveable items such as shrouds and stays.

RIGGING SCREW. A device fitted between the stay or shroud and hull to apply tension to the rigging. *See* Bottle Screw, Open Frame Rigging Screw.

RIGHT HANDED PROPELLOR. One that turns clockwise when viewed from the stern.

RIGHT HANDED ROPE. Rope in which the strands spiral to the right.

RIGHT OF WAY. A vessel on a certain course has legal right of way over another vessel. Basic laws are illustrated on opposite page.

RIGHT THE HELM. Put the rudder amidships.

RINGBOLT. A bolt with a loose fitting ring in one end for the attaching of blocks, etc.

RING TAIL. An extra sail that is set abaft the spanker. Was used by the heavy racing skiffs early this century, notably in Sydney Harbour, Australia.

RISINGS. The stringers placed in a boat to support the thwarts.

ROACH. Curvature of the foot of a square sail. 2. Curvature of the luff of a headsail.

ROADSTEAD. An area where a vessel will find fair anchorage and shelter.

ROARING FORTIES. A belt of strong westerlies which prevail south of latitude 40 degrees.

ROBAND. Short lengths of rope fixed around the headrope of a squaresail and used to attach it to the jackstay.

ROCKERED. Said of a keel that, in profile, is not straight.

ROCKETS. Distress signals which are sent into the air by igniting powder in the base. They display various shapes and colours to attract attention.

ROLLER FAIRLEAD. A fairlead whose base consists of a roller over which cable runs freely. Typically used at the bow. *See* Anchor Roller

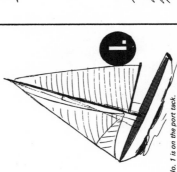

RIGHT OF WAY.

Power

No. 3 gives way to No. 4, passes No. 1 to port and stands on for No. 2.

No. 2 gives way to No. 3, stands on for Nos. 1 and 4 because she is to their right.

No. 4 stands on for No. 3 and gives way to Nos. 1 and 2.

No. 1 gives way to No. 2, stands on for No. 4 and passes No. 3 to port.

The laws relating to motor vessels are easier to remember than those for sailing vessels because wind direction is not considered. Basically, the rule states that you give way to the right where two vessels' paths are about to cross. When approaching head on, both vessels move to the right so that they pass each other on the porthand side.

Sailing

The laws relating to sailing vessels can be briefly summed up as follows; those with the wind over the starboard side, and are thus on a starboard tack, have right of way over those on the port tack. Windward vessels give way to leeward vessels. More intricate details are shown below.

No. 2 is on the starboard tack. Stands on for all other boats because Nos. 1, 4 and 5 are on the port tack and No. 3, although with the wind on the same side, is to windward.

No. 1 is on the port tack. Keeps clear of Nos. 2 and 3 as they are on the starboard tack. Stands on for Nos. 4 and 5 as they are also on the port tack and are to windward.

No. 3 is on the starboard tack. Keeps clear of No. 2 because she is to leeward. Stands on for Nos. 1, 4 and 5 because they are on the port tack.

No. 4 is on the port tack because her mainsail is carried to starboard. Keeps clear of all boats because Nos. 1 and 5 are to leeward and Nos. 2 and 3 are on the starboard tack.

No. 5 is on the port tack. Keeps clear of No. 1 because she is to leeward on the same tack. Keeps clear of Nos. 2 and 3 because they are on the starboard tack. Stands on for No. 4 because she is to weather and is on the same tack.

Wind

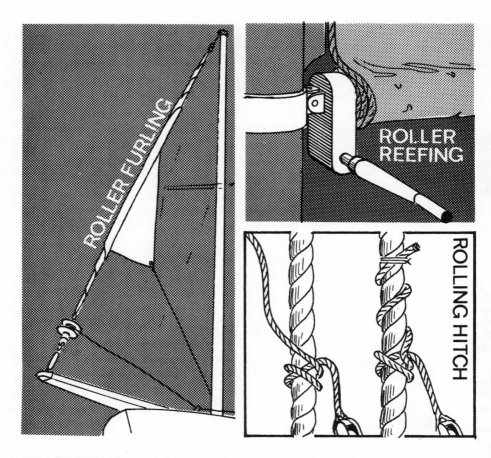

ROLLER FURLING. A fairly recent innovation used for the furling or reefing of a headsail. The headsail's luffwire has a swivel at the top and a swivel and reel at the bottom. A line permanently wound around this reel, when pulled, will wind the sail around its luffwire. When released and the sheet is pulled, the sail will unwind. It is more a furling system than a reefing system but momentary reefing can be achieved during a bad gust.

ROLLER REEFING. A method of reducing the area of a boomed mainsail by winding it down around the boom like an upside-down blind. There are many types but the principle is the same. Namely, a handle is turned which rotates the boom which pulls the mainsail down and around it. The method is streamlined but suffers from the fact that the end of the boom tends to sag giving the sail very poor setting qualities once reefed.

ROLLING CHOCK OR CLEAT. Alternative name for a 'bilge keel' when its primary purpose is to dampen roll. *See* Bilge Keel.

ROLLING HITCH. A hitch made as shown. Valuable when a line must be made fast to a shroud, stay or rail yet must not slip along same.

ROOMING. Opening the distance off a lee shore. To 'make rooming' is to work offshore until at a safe distance.

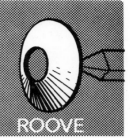

ROOVES. Small 'washers' of copper that fit over the end of copper nails inside a wooden boat and are held by burring the nail over.

ROOVING IRON. A tool used for holding a roove over the end of a nail.

ROPE. Lengths of wire, manilla, cotton, synthetics, etc. laid up into right handed yarns which are twisted into left handed strands and the strands are laid up into right handed rope (normally). A rope is anything over one inch circumference. Under that size it is called a 'line'.

ROUGH LOG. The deck log. A journal of shipboard events.

ROUND HEAD SCREW. An ordinary wood screw with a half sphere head.

ROUND SEIZING. A seizing made as shown. Ideal where the strain on both rope ends are in the same direction.

ROUND TURN. A complete turn of rope around a bitt.

ROUND TURN AND TWO HALF HITCHES. A simple knot as shown. Ideal when making fast to a ring.

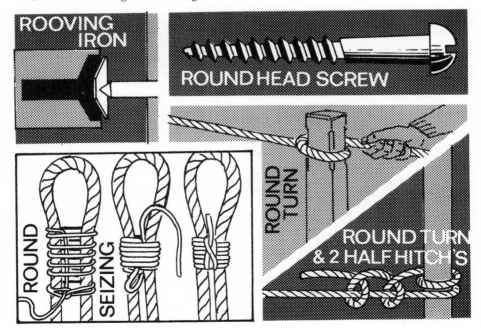

ROUND UP. To close the space between two blocks of a tackle after it has been extended. 2. To turn the vessel's bow into the wind. Typically when drifting up to a mooring or anchorage.

ROVE. Past tense of 'reeve'. When a rope has been passed through a block it has been 'rove'. 2. Alternative spelling to 'roove'.

ROW. To move a boat by pulling oars.

ROW BOAT. Any boat propelled by oars.

ROWLOCK. A crutch fitted into the gunwhale of a row boat to accommodate the oar.

ROYAL. Sail immediately above topgallant. *See illustration of full rigged ship, page 5.*

ROYAL MAST. Mast above topgallant mast. *See illustration, page* 116

RUBBING PIECE OR STRAKE. Sacrificial beading along outside of hull near the sheerline to take chafing when alongside.

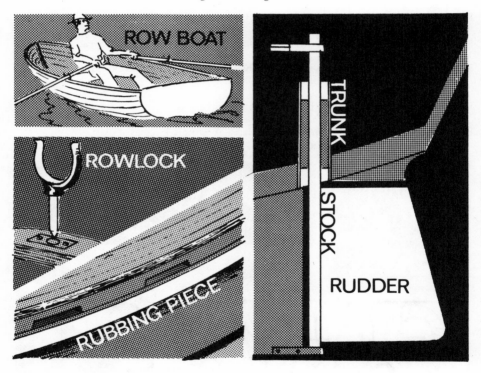

RUDDER. The device used for steering.

RUDDER STOCK. The 'axle' to which rudder plate is attached.

RUDDER TRUNK. The casing in the hull through which the rudder enters.

RULE OF THE ROAD. Officially known as 'Regulations for Preventing Collisions at Sea'.

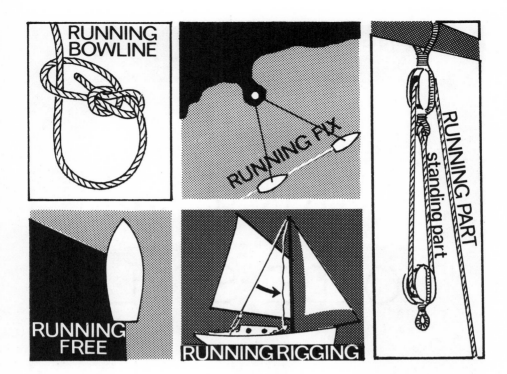

RUMBOLINE. Condemned rope used for lashing where strength is not of great importance. Sometimes called 'rumbo'.

RUNNING BOWLINE. As shown, a bowline tied around its standing part and used as a noose.

RUNNING FIX. Taking a bearing from an object ashore, sailing a known distance along a known course, then taking a second bearing from the same object to establish position. Only sensible if severe drift is suspected.

RUNNING FREE. Sailing with the wind anywhere aft of about 60 degrees from the bow. More generally accepted as describing a vessel sailing with the wind somewhere abaft the beam.

RUNNING LIGHTS. Navigational lights displayed by a vessel when under way. *See* Navigation Lights.

RUNNING PART. Any part of a tackle that moves as against the part that remains stationary.

RUNNING RIGGING. Any rigging aboard ship used to work or hoist sails etc. For example, sheets and halyards, dinghy hoist and so on.

RUNNING STAY. A stay which must be set up and tensioned every time the weight of wind in a sail demands. Commonly the mainsail demands that a running backstay be set up. Very rarely, a running forestay is used as insurance against a backing square sail imparting more pressure than the standing stays can withstand. Methods of tensioning a running stay vary from the simple handy-billy to the Highfield Lever.
See Highfield Lever.

Sail Parts

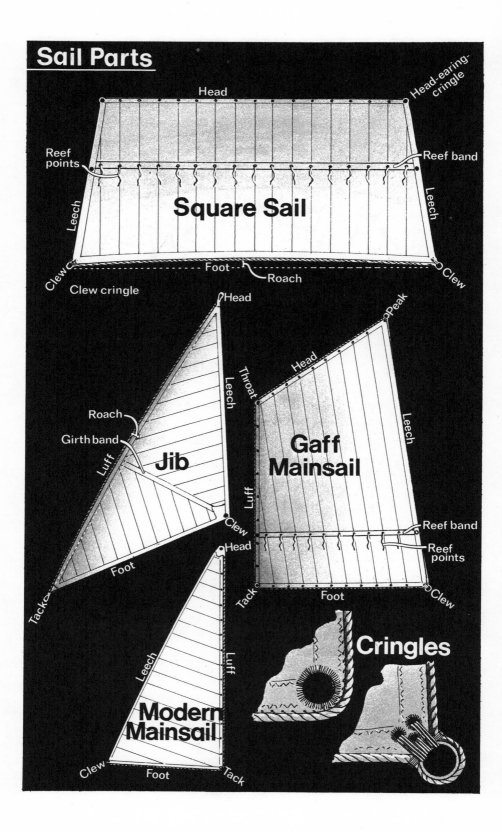

Square Sail

Head

Head-earing-cringle

Reef points

Reef band

Leech

Leech

Clew

Clew

Foot

Roach

Clew cringle

Jib

Head

Leech

Roach

Girth band

Luff

Clew

Foot

Tack

Gaff Mainsail

Peak

Head

Throat

Leech

Luff

Reef band

Reef points

Tack

Foot

Clew

Modern Mainsail

Head

Leech

Luff

Clew

Foot

Tack

Cringles

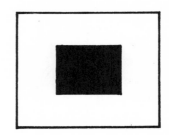

S. Flag of the International Code of Signals meaning; 'My engines are going astern.' White background with blue oblong centre.

SADDLE. Any wooden or metal chock whose sole purpose is to support a part of the rig. For example, boom gallows have a saddle in which sits the boom; a jib-boom sits into a saddle on the bowsprit, etc.

SAFE WORKING LOAD. Abbreviated S.W.L. The limit to which any tackle can be extended whilst remaining within a safety factor. With rope the SWL tends to be about one sixth the actual breaking strain. To find the size rope required to lift a given load, the square root of the load in cwts. will give the rope size (in inches circumference) required.

SAG. To drift to leeward. To 'sag' downwind.

SAIL. Any canvas or synthetic fabric spread to catch the wind and drive a vessel along. As shown opposite, there are many types with further variation in the method of cutting. Sails fall into two basic categories; standing sails and extras. Standing sails are those that make up the basic rig. On a sloop, this would be jib and mainsail. Extras are those sails set to keep the vessel moving at optimum speed during light weather such as the spinnaker or, in bad weather, a trysail.

SAIL COVER. Canvas or synthetic fibre cover placed over the sails when still attached to the spars but not in use. Ideally, they should permit a flow of air around the sails.

SAIL LOFT. A large flat floor space where sails are measured and cut.

SAILMAKER. Person trained in the art of making sails.

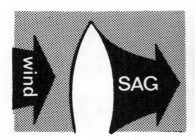

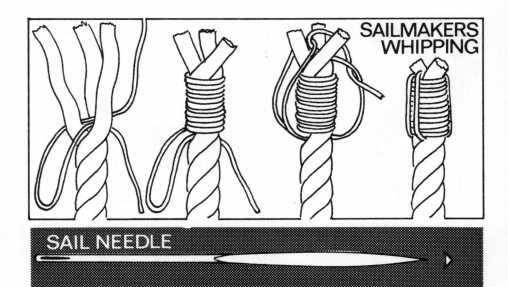

SAILMAKERS WHIPPING

SAIL NEEDLE

SAILMAKER'S WHIPPING. The best of all whippings. It is made as shown. Open the strands of the rope and lay the line with a loop loosely around one strand and a long and a short end projecting opposite. Lay up the rope strands again then put on the whipping turns. When these are on bring the loop up and outside the whipping and place it around the strand it is already encircling. Bring the short end up and tie it to the long end at the centre of the rope.

SAIL NEEDLE. A special needle used in sail making. The pointed end is triangular in section.

SAILOR. One who sails aboard any type of ship, be it power driven or sail.

SAIL TRACK. A track along the back of the mast into which fits track slides with the luff of the mainsail attached. There are many variations on the theme, including internal and external track, as shown, but their purpose remains the same.

SALINITY. The amount of dissolved salt in water.

SALOON. Traditionally the mess room for deck officers. Contemporarily, it is used by yachtsmen to describe the lounging area aboard a small boat. Usually is equipped with dining table and settee berths.

SAMSON POST. Any post well seated and of massive proportions to take excessive loads. Aboard small craft it is the forward bitt. *See* Bitts.

SAIL TRACK

SANDBAGGER. An early racing boat which used bags of sand for ballast. The bags were moved up to the windward side every time it changed tacks. Many of the early sailing fishing boats also employed this method of ballasting when empty. They would sail to the fishing grounds in sand ballast, then progressively dump the sand as the hold filled with fish.

SANDBANK. Any shoal area of a waterway caused by a collection of sand.

SASH EYE. Small eye fixed to a plate which can be screwed into position. Also called 'deck eye'.

SASH HOOK. An identical fitting to the sash eye except for the open eye forming a hook. Also called 'deck hook'.

SAXBOARD. The top strake of an open boat. The 'sheer strake'.

SCANNER. The rotating head of a radar set. Beams are transmitted and received by this head.

SCANTLINGS. The measurements of structural members, whether timber or otherwise, used in the construction of a boat.

SCARF. A method of joining two pieces of timber or steel as shown. Can be spelt 'scarph'.

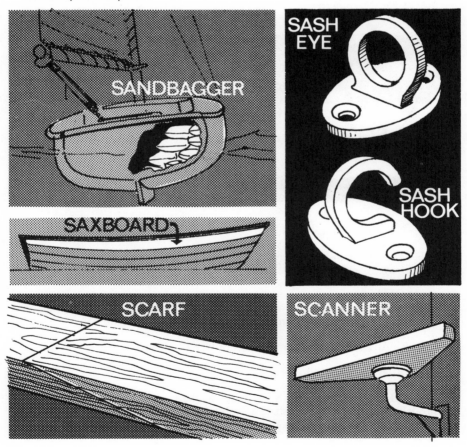

SCEND. When under way at sea, the upward rising of the bow area when the stern falls into a trough.

SCHOONER. A fore and aft rigged vessel with two or more masts. When two masted, the after mast is always taller than the foremast. When three masted the masts can be of varying heights but commonly they are similar. For various schooner rigs, see page 9. One of the first schooners was built by Andrew Robinson at Gloucester, Massachusetts in 1713. Legend has it that when the vessel was launched and sailing, a spectator cried out; "There she scoons". Scoon is New England dialect meaning to skim across the water.

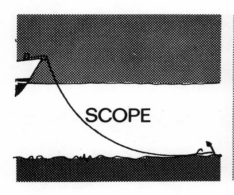

SCOPE. The amount of cable laid out between the ship and her anchor.

SCORE. The groove in a block to take the strop. *See* Common Block *illustration.*

SCOTCH MIST. Light, misty rain.

SCOW. Flat bottomed, square ended craft, used mostly as a dumb barge.

SCRAPER. Any tool used to scrape paint or weed and barnacles.

SCREW. Alternative name for propellor.

SCREW ALLEY. Nickname for 'shaft alley' or 'shaft tunnel'. Is the tunnel through which the propellor shaft of a ship passes, giving access for maintenance and oiling crews and separating cargo and accommodation areas from the shaft.

SCUDDING. To run fast before a strong wind.

SCULL. To propel a boat along using one oar — or 'scull', over the stern.
Fitted to a notch to prevent it jumping out, the scull is moved from side
to side in a rhythmic motion turning the blade at the end of each stroke
so that it forces water away from the stern.

SCUPPER. Hole in bulwarks or toe rail to allow water to flow off the deck.

SCUTTLE. Essentially, this is an alternative name for a porthole, it being
an opening in the side of a hull to admit light and air. 2. The act of
purposely sinking — 'scuttling' a ship by opening a cock underwater.

SEA ANCHOR. Any object or collection of objects streamed to windward
to slow down the leeward rush of a vessel in heavy weather. A true
sea anchor is a canvas open-ended cone which is streamed on the end of
a line from a bridle as shown. Under practical conditions the sea anchor
tends to be insufficient or it readily carries away. One of the best
alternatives is a collection of floorboards, fenders and tyres lashed
together and streamed. Long bights of rope and chain with nothing
attached can also serve to slow the vessel down.

SEA BREEZE. A wind blowing onto the land from the sea.

SEA COCK. A valve through which sea water is admitted into the bilge, or into the engine's cooling system.

SEA KINDLY. Said of a hull with few vices and a general compatibility with the sea. A comfortable vessel in rough weather.

SEA LEGS. Ability to walk along a tossing deck without being thrown.

SEAMAN. Any person who puts to sea.

SEAMANSHIP. The art of handling all facets of a vessel.

SEA ROOM. Sufficient space to manoeuvre a vessel without risking collision or grounding.

SEAWORTHY. Said of a vessel in fair condition and able to put to sea with little fear of her 'working' or breaking up.

SECRET FASTENED DECK. A method of laying deck planks so that no fastenings are visible. Each plank is diagonally nailed into the beam as well as being nailed into the neighbouring plank.

SEIZING. A means of binding two ropes together to keep them secure. The most popular ones are shown throughout this book under their various headings. *See* Racking Seizing, Round Seizing, Flat Seizing, etc.

SELF BAILER. A venturi tube fitted to the bottom of a small skiff that reaches speeds fast enough to create a sucking action which draws water out from the bilge. When the speed is too slow and water might enter, a bung is inserted from inside. A more modern device which creates less drag when not in use is the 'trapdoor bailer' or 'retractable drainer'. *See illustration on page 221.*

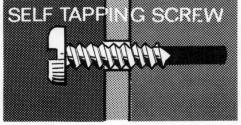

SELF TAPPING SCREW. A special screw of either mild steel or stainless steel whose thread is well defined and of constant diameter that will force a mating thread in a plain undersize hole. Ideal for fastening any sheeting material to steel frames, etc.

SEMI ROTARY PUMP. One of the original types of pumps employed aboard boats. Still popular for fuel delivery. *See illustration on page* 220.

SENNITS. Essentially a sennit is a fancy display in rope made by plaiting rope, rope strands, yarns, etc. There are many types, including the Common, Double Carrick, English, French, Railway, Russian, Thrum, etc. The Common and French Sennits are illustrated.

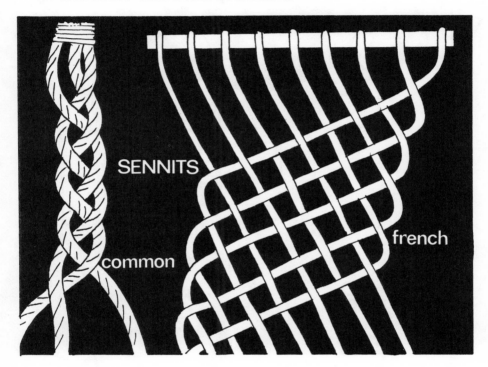

SENNITS

common

french

SERVE. To cover a rope with marline or similar to hold the parcelling in place and to unite with the parcelling as a protection to the rope against moisture penetration, chafe, etc. Because it is a similar treatment to whipping, the two terms are often confused. A whipping, as explained under its own heading, does not require parcelling under it and is more a short 'serve' at the end of the rope to prevent it unlaying. The tying off of a serve or whipping does, however, tend to be identical.

SERVING MALLET. A mallet, as shown, for the sole purpose of serving a rope. The mallet is rotated around the rope with the marline feeding off it under the control of the hand holding the mallet.

SET. Direction in which a current flows.

SET AND DRIFT. The direction and distance that a current travels in a given time.

219.

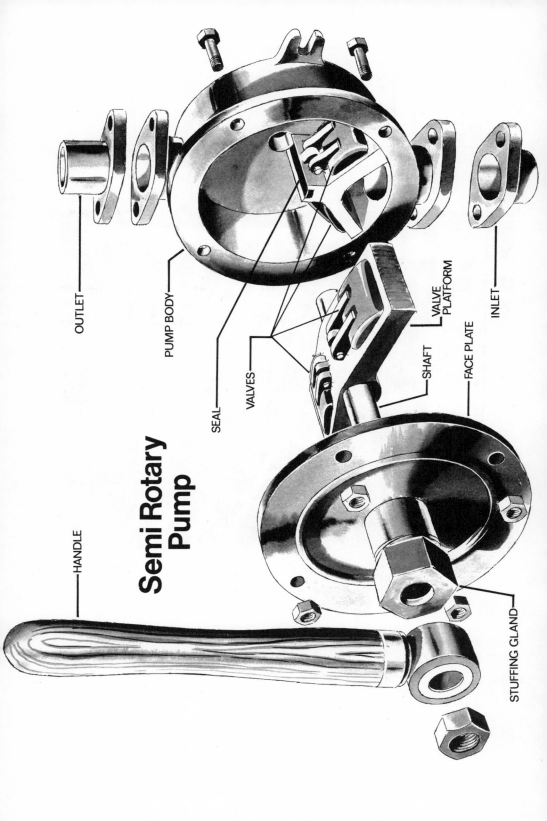

Semi Rotary Pump

HANDLE

OUTLET

PUMP BODY

SEAL

VALVES

VALVE PLATFORM

SHAFT

FACE PLATE

INLET

STUFFING GLAND

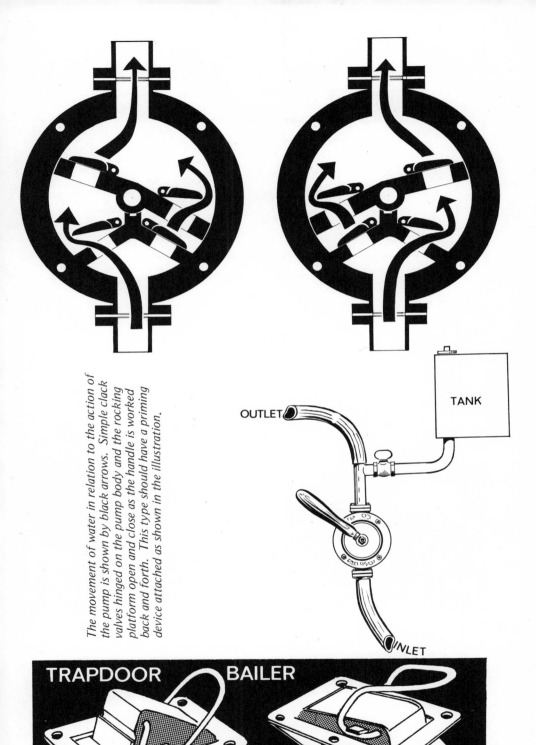

The movement of water in relation to the action of the pump is shown by black arrows. Simple clack valves hinged on the pump body and the rocking platform open and close as the handle is worked back and forth. This type should have a priming device attached as shown in the illustration.

TANK

OUTLET

INLET

TRAPDOOR BAILER

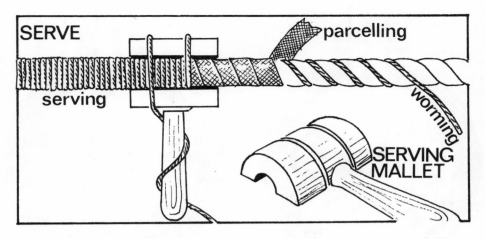

SET SAIL. To bend on and hoist sail. To leave harbour.

SETTEE RIG. Broadly speaking this is an alternative name for 'gaff rig'.

SEXTANT. A navigational instrument for measuring angles. Primarily used to measure the angle between a celestial body and the earth's horizon, but can also be used in coastal navigation for measuring vertical angles between the shoreline and the top of a lighthouse or tower or horizontally between headlands, etc.

SHACKLE. A 'U' shaped bar of steel having an eye in each end through which passes a pin. There are many different types but all have the same function of joining two items together such as chain to anchor, shrouds to plates, etc.

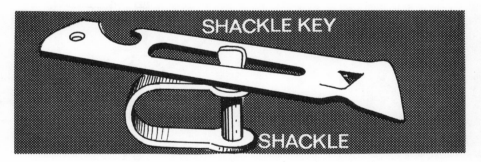

SHACKLE KEY. A special tool for undoing and tightening shackles. Usually combined with a bottle opener and can spanner.

SHAFT. Any transmission shaft. Primarily the propellor shaft.

SHAFT ALLEY. *See* Screw Alley.

SHAFT LOG. *See* Stuffing Box.

SHAKEDOWN CRUISE. The first cruise of a vessel's or crew's experience. The time when things and people are 'shaken down' into an efficient, functioning team.

Micrometer Sextant

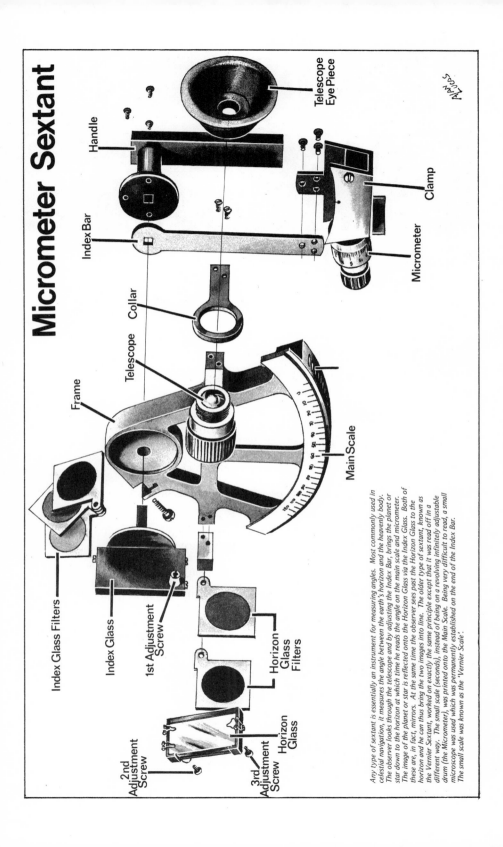

Telescope Eye Piece

Handle

Clamp

Index Bar

Micrometer

Collar

Telescope

Frame

Main Scale

Index Glass Filters

Index Glass

1st Adjustment Screw

Horizon Glass Filters

2nd Adjustment Screw

3rd Adjustment Screw

Horizon Glass

Any type of sextant is essentially an instrument for measuring angles. Most commonly used in celestial navigation, it measures the angle between the earth's horizon and the heavenly body. The observer looks through the telescope and by adjusting the Index Bar, brings the planet or star down to the horizon at which time he reads the angle on the main scale and micrometer. The image of the planet or star is reflected onto the Horizon Glass via the Index Glass. Both of these are, in fact, mirrors. At the same time the observer sees past the Horizon Glass to the horizon and he can thus bring the two images into line. The older type of sextant, known as the Vernier Sextant, worked on exactly the same principle except that it was read off in a different way. The small scale (seconds), instead of being on a revolving infinitely adjustable drum (the Micrometer), was printed onto the Main Scale. Being very difficult to read, a small microscope was used which was permanently established on the end of the Index Bar. The small scale was known as the 'Vernier Scale'.

SHAKE OUT A REEF. To take out a reef of a sail. To increase sail area again after heavy weather.

SHAMROCK KNOT. A knot tied as shown and commonly used to take the stays and shrouds of a temporarily rigged mast. Also called a 'jury mast knot'.

SHANK. The part of an anchor between the flukes and the ring.
See Admiralty Pattern Anchor *illustration.*

SHARPIE. Tradionally a long, narrow flat-bottomed sailing boat. Is often used to describe any hard chine boat, regardless of its propulsion.

SHEATHING. A layer of copper or extra planks on the outside of a hull's bottom to help prevent growth or act as a sacrificial skin for ship worms, etc. *See also* Copper Sheathing.

SHEAVE. The 'wheel' in a block. *See* Common Block *illustration.*

SHEER. The upward sweep of the deckline from amidships to fore and aft. The 'sheerline'.

SHEER LEGS. Two poles lashed together at the top and splayed out at the bottom from which a tackle can be hung to lift heavy objects.

SHEER RAIL. The lowest plank in the bulwark planking.

SHEER STRAKE. The top plank, or strake, of a hull. The one closest to the deckline.

SHEET. A rope attached to the clew of a sail and used to control it. Part of the running rigging.

SHEET ANCHOR. A third bower anchor. Usually stowed amidships because it should be the heaviest anchor aboard for use in bad anchorages during deteriorating weather. Thus the saying; 'have a sheet anchor to windward', meaning, have maximum security or insurance.

SHEET BEND. An ideal knot for joining ropes of unequal thickness. It is formed as shown, always being careful to form the first bight in the larger of the two ropes. The right-hand illustration shows a double sheet bend used when the rope is wet or there is considerable difference in rope size.

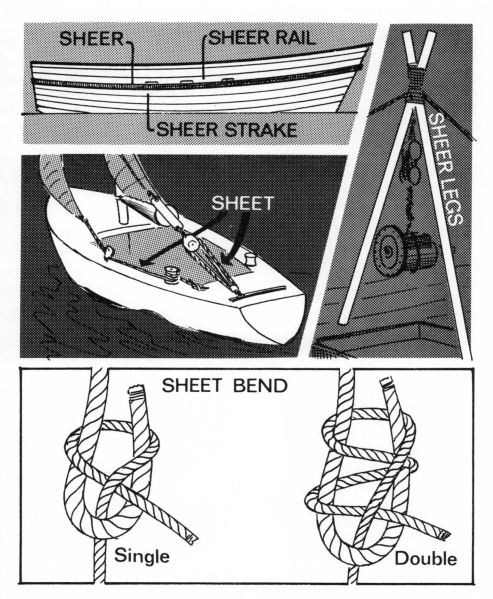

SHEER · SHEER RAIL

SHEER STRAKE

SHEET

SHEERLEGS

SHEET BEND

Single · Double

SHEET HOME. To haul in the sheets and thus pull the sail until it is taut and hard in. An action when coming hard onto the wind.

SHELF. A strong length of timber which bolts around the perimeter of the hull to impart strength and give a landing for the deck beams. Thus the term 'deck shelf'. The clamp can do a similar job but often the one shelf or clamp does the job of both. *See* Clamp *illustration.*

SHELL. The outside planking or skin of a hull. 2. A racing rowing skiff. 3. The case of a block. *See* Common Block.

SHELLBACK. An old experienced seaman.

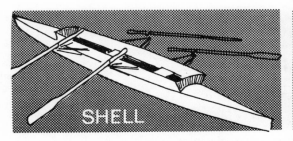

SHELL VENTILATOR. A low profile cowling designed to scoop air through the hole it embraces.

SHINGLE. Coarse gravel that has been smoothed by the action of the sea.

SHIP. Strictly speaking, a sailing vessel with three or more masts, each mast carrying squaresails. Can now mean any vessel large enough to accommodate crew below decks, but more generally used to describe vessels of over 100 feet.

SHIPBROKER. One who buys and sells boats or acts as an agent between vendor and purchaser.

SHIP CHANDLER. One who deals in supplying ships with commodities from boat hardware to food and drink.

SHIP RIGGED. Square rigged on all masts if they number three or more.

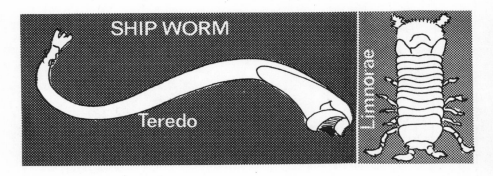

SHIP WORM. A misnomer for the mollusc *teredo* which destroys timber by eating the cellulose. Together with another destroyer of timber, the *limnorae*, it is one of the few creatures able to digest this material. The teredo bores into its future underwater home starting as an infant so small as to be difficult to see, then enlarges its living quarters as growth demands. Its rudimentary shells are placed on the back of the head and are the tunnelling tools. Timber quickly becomes hollow and structurally useless. The limnorae differs from the teredo in every way, being a different genus, size and appearance. It lives close to the surface of the wood and does only localised damage. It too, is misnamed 'ship worm' occasionally.

SHORE. A strong prop used to support a vessel or other object when natural support is removed.

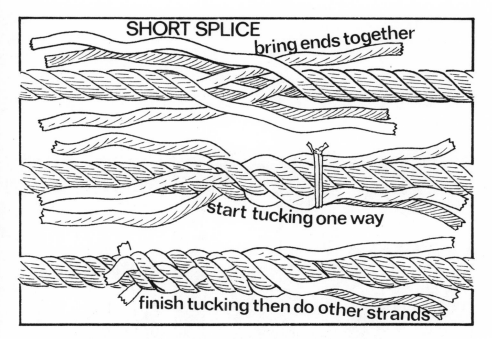

SHORT SPLICE — bring ends together — start tucking one way — finish tucking then do other strands

SHORT SPLICE. A method of joining two ropes to make one continuous length. It cannot be run through a block unless the block is oversize.

SHORT STAY. Said of a vessel's anchor cable when the amount of cable is of a length of not more than one and a half times the depth of water.

SHOULDER BLOCK. A block with a piece added to shell to hold it off the mast to prevent rope binding.

SHROUD. The rigging that supports a mast against athwartship movement.

SHROUD BRIDLE. A cringle or similar object seized to a shroud to confine halyards, etc.

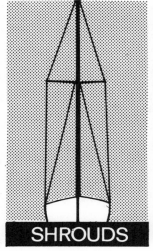

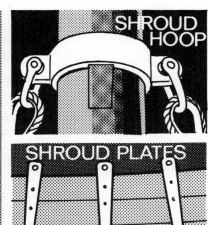

SHROUDS

SHROUD BRIDLE

SHROUD HOOP

SHROUD PLATES

SHROUD HOOP. A collar of steel around the mast to take the top ends of the outer shrouds. Specifically names a collar taking only shrouds but can also be called a 'mast band' as described and illustrated under that heading.

SHROUD KNOT. This was used in the days when shrouds were made of rope. When one had been shot away in battle, it was rejoined by bringing the two ends together as in the start of a short splice but were tied off in the form of a Wall Knot. The ends were then tapered down and served.

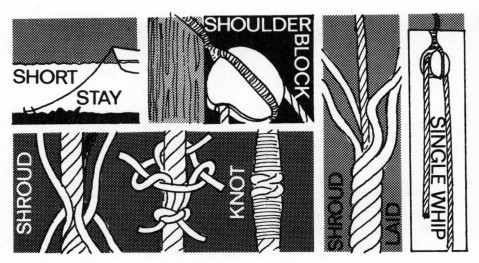

SHROUD LAID. A four strand rope with a separate centre heart laid hawser fashion (either left-hand or right-hand lay where the yarns are laid in the opposite direction to the lay).

SHROUD PLATES. Metal plates fastened through the hull either from inside or outside which take the lower ends of the shrouds. A tensioning device, such as a rigging screw, is always fitted between the shrouds and their plates.

SIDE LIGHTS. The red and green navigational lights *See* Navigation Lights.

SILICONE BRONZE. An alloy of silica and copper with traces of tin and antimony used for boat parts, especially boat nails.

SILVER ROPE. Of the polyethylene family. Originally developed to replace float ropes such as coir, which it did with great success. Has proved an ideal all-round boat rope for anchoring, sheets and halyards. Silver rope is one of the few synthetic ropes which has the added advantage of having a rough surface making it easy to grip and resistant to chafe.

SINGLE WHIP. Rope led through a single standing block for hoisting. No mechanical advantage is enjoyed.

SISAL. The fibre from leaves of the agave from Indonesia and Africa. Before synthetics it was the most popular general use rope although manilla was always preferable aboard ship.

SISTER BLOCK. Two sheaves one above the other in the same shell. *See* Fiddle Block.

SISTER HOOK. A fast method of uniting two lines, etc., as illustrated here and described under heading 'Clip Hooks'.

SKARTSEN SCRAPER. The trade name of a special type of paint-scraper which employs a removable re-sharpenable head.

SKEG. A bracket fitted to the keel or planking to support the propellor shaft bearing. 2. A vertical surface in front of the rudder.

SKENE CHOCK or FAIRLEAD. *See* Continental Fairlead.

SKIFF. A small light boat either decked or open and propelled by oars, sail or outboard motor.

SKIN. The outside plating or planking of a hull. If it is double planked, it is the inside layer.

SKIN FITTING. A through-hull fitting which admits and expels water for such items as toilet, galley and washbasins.

SKIPPER. Loosely applied to any ship's master but specifically applies to the master of a fishing boat.

SKI TOW HOOK. A simple, easily released hook for attaching to the ski rope when towing.

SKYLIGHT

SLAMMING

SKYLIGHT. Glass opening to provide light and air through deck. Traditionally hinged fore and aft, but more adaptable as a hatch type with loose lid.

SKYSAIL. An extra squaresail set above the royal yard. *See* Moonsail *illustration.*

SLAB SIDED. Said of any high sided vessel.

SLACK WATER. Said of the time at high or low tide when no run is apparent.

SLAMMING. The action of a vessel slapping the waves as she pushes into a headsea. Most common on shoal draught, beamy vessels and especially hard chine planing hulls.

SLATTING. The fairly slow rhythmic beating of sails against shipboard objects when becalmed.

SLEEPERS. Knees connecting transom to the hull planking or stringers.

SLIDING KEEL. Alternative name for 'drop keel' or 'dagger board'.

SLIP KNOT. Any knot made up in such a way that the knot can be yanked apart, regardless of the loading.

SLIPSTREAM. The current of water directed around the rudder by the propellor.

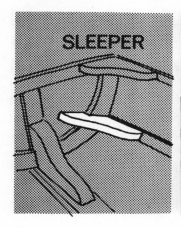

SLEEPER

SLIDING KEEL

SLIP KNOT

SLIPWAY. A marine railway designed to haul boats out of the water.

SLOOP. A one-masted vessel with one jib and one mainsail. Originally could mean a one masted vessel with bowsprit and up to three headsails if one was a topsail. This type is now called a 'cutter'.

SLOPS. The rubbish from the galley.

SMACK. Originally a sloop or cutter rigged vessel. Now tends to apply only to semi decked sailing fishing boats.

SMALL BOWER. The port bower (bow) anchor used in light weather.

SNAP HOOK. A self mousing hook as shown.

SNAP SHACKLE. Similar to the snap hook except that the 'hook' itself hinges back to accept or release a line. A more reliable type.

SNATCH BLOCK. A block giving access to the swallow from the side. Some have a hinged plate here to trap the rope.

SNOTTER. A general-use strop for supporting objects such as a spinnaker pole against the mast on skiffs as shown.

SNOW. Brig-rigged vessel whose driver is bent on to a small mast close abaft the mainmast.

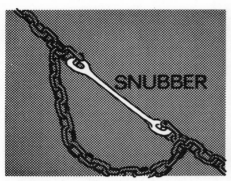 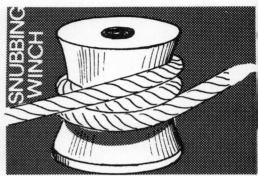

SNUB. To suddenly check anything running out.

SNUBBER. A cable stopper. In modern terminology it means a shock absorbing length of rubber shackled to the anchor cable.

SNUBBING WINCH. One used to grab the slack of a line as the weight alternatively comes on and off. Has no handle.

 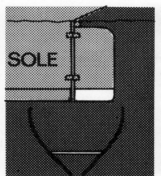 

SOFT LAID. A rope that has been loosely laid up to give it softness and flexibility. Most ropes are soft or semi soft laid.

SOLDIER'S WIND. A beam wind. So named because it is the easiest course on which to steer a boat and thus 'even a soldier' could steer her.

SOLE. A removable piece attached to the heel of a rudder. It gives greater area yet can be removed when the vessel goes on the hard to avoid unnecessary weight coming to bear on the rudder. Although seldom officially stated as such, the word 'sole' has also come to mean the cabin floor. Thus, 'cabin sole'.

SOLID THIMBLE. A thimble with only a hole through which to fasten it. For maximum strength.

SONIC SOUNDER. *See* Echo Sounder.

SOUND. A narrow expanse of water between two land masses. 2. The act of checking the depth with lead line or echo sounder. 3. Said of a hull in good condition. 4. Denotes the action of a whale plunging rapidly into deeper water.

SPANISH BURTON. A method of rigging blocks and tackle as shown.

SPANISH REEF. A quick, sloppy method of reefing a sail, regardless of how it is done. A headsail can be reduced by tying the head as shown or a mainsail can be 'reefed' by dropping it then tying the clew.

SPANISH WINDLASS. A highly effective method of heaving two parts together. Extremely handy in boat building when forcing planks home, etc.

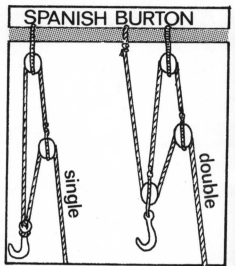

SPANKER. Fore and aft sail with gaff and boom set from the after mast of a ship or barque. *See* Full Rigged Ship *illustration, page 5*

SPANKING PACE. Means a cracking pace. Fast. Exciting.

SPAR. Name of any yard, gaff, boom or mast.

SPECTACLES. Figure of eight clew irons attached to a sail when chain sheets are used.

SPENCER. Loose footed trysail attached to gaff as shown.

SPIDER BAND. A collar around mast fitted with belaying pins or cleats.

SPIKE BOWSPRIT. A single bowsprit combining the function of bowsprit and jib boom.

SPILE. A wooden pin to plug nail holes, etc.

SPINNAKER. A large extra sail used in light to moderate weather when the wind is abaft the beam. Usually a balloon type, but can also be flat.

SPINNAKER POLE. A spar to spread the foot of the spinnaker. It clips on to the mast a little above deck at one end, the other end clipping onto one of the spinnaker's clews.

SPINNAKER POLE END. A fitting on each end of the spinnaker pole which is remote controlled by a lanyard for clipping it onto mast and sail.

SPINNAKER POLE MAST RING. A fitting with either one or two eyes attached into which the spinnaker pole is clipped.

SPITFIRE JIB. Name of small storm jib.

SPLICE. Intertwining rope back into its own lay to effect a connection.
See Eye Splice, Long Splice and Short Splice.

SPLINE PLANKING. A method of sealing the seams between the planks of
a carvel built hull using a tapered spline. It is glued then hammered into
the seam. When the glue hardens the excess spline is planed down.
It provides an ideal method of renovating an old hull whose seams are
so wide as to deny effective caulking.

SPLIT BACKSTAY. Where a single backstay runs from the masthead down
to a point above deck where it becomes twin backstays to embrace the
cockpit area or a mizzen mast.

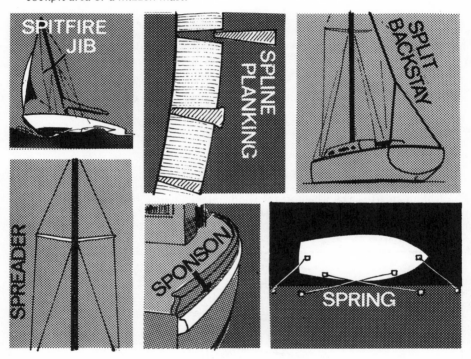

SPONSON. The wide rubbing strip or belting around a hull at or near
deck level. Is often called 'gunwale'. Was originally name of projection
on which a gun was carried outboard.

SPREADER. Alternative name for cross-trees in the modern sense.

SPRING. A rope taken from the stern and led forward or from the bow
and led aft to warp the ship fore or aft by its own winches. When berthed,
identical line placement prevents the ship wandering or fetching under
the wharf decking. Springs also present a means of getting off the wharf
without outside assistance. It is done by letting all lines go except for
the forward spring then steaming ahead with rudder hard over to kick the
stern out. The vessel is then put astern and the spring thrown off.

SPRING TIDES. When the range between high and low water levels is
greatest. They occur around full and new moon.

SPRIT. A boom set diagonally across a four sided fore and aft 'sprit' sail.

SPRUNG. Said of a mast when excessive strains have caused a fracture. Often used to describe a hull that has spewed its caulking after suffering damage.

SPURLING PIPE. Alternative name for 'navel pipe'. *See* Navel Pipe.

SQUARE KNOT. A knot formed as shown. Can be used to interlace two ropes crossing at right angles or as a means of uniting two ends which pull from right angles.

SQUARE RIG. Where the sails are bent to yards which lie across the ship. An athwartships rig as against a fore and aft rig. Square rig enjoys maximum efficiency when off the wind and minimum efficiency when close hauled. Fore and aft sails have the opposite characteristics.

SQUARE SAIL. *For details see illustration opposite 'sail'.*

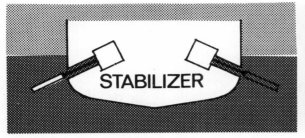 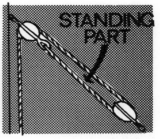

STABILIZER. A mechanical device working a pair of fins which, against the forward motion of the vessel, tend to resist the rolling moment.

STAINLESS STEEL. An alloy of steel, chromium and nickel. It is designated by three digit numbers which indicate the type's hardening process and potential durability. Essentially, two hardening processes are used; one, by heating and quenching; two, by cold working (hammer blows or similar). When the first digit is *even* it is hardened by cold working. When the number is *odd* it is hardened by heating and quenching. 316 is the most suitable for marine use, having ample strength and corrosion resistance, but not necessarily the maximum of either field.

STANDING LUG. Same as the 'dipping lug' except that the sail remains on one side of the mast regardless of which tack it is sailing on. *See* Dipping Lug *illustration.*

STANDING PART. That part of the tackle which is made fast to the block or object and does not move.

STANDING RIGGING. That rigging employed in supporting the mast or spars. Rigging that does not move except by normal and acceptable strains.

STAND ON. Maintain course and speed.

STARBOARD. The right-hand side of the vessel, looking forward.

STARBOARD TACK. Sailing with the wind blowing over the starboard side.

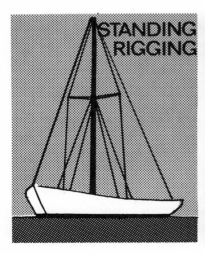  

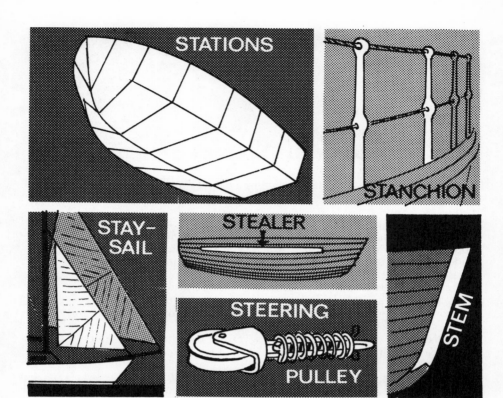

STATEROOM. The owner's or special guest's cabin. Usually has own
head (toilet).

STATIONS. The frame sections of the hull.

STAUNCHION. The handrail supports.

STAYS. That part of the standing rigging which prevents the masts from
moving fore and aft. *See* Standing Rigging.

STAYSAIL. A headsail which hanks onto a stay and is often named after
that stay. In modern terminology the staysail is often the one hanked onto
the inner forestay. Those on other forestays being called jib,
genoa or outer jib.

STEALER. A tapering length of plank fitted between other strakes to
compensate for the narrowing effect of the hull shape.

STEERING PULLEY. A sprung loaded pulley used in conjunction with
wheel steering.

STEM. The timber at the bow into which the strakes fit and terminate.

STEM FITTING. Loose term describing a fitting over the stem head which
usually takes the forestay and can sometimes have a bowsprit band
and anchor-roller incorporated into its construction. Also called 'Stem Cap'.

STEM HEAD. The upper extremity of the stem.

STEMMING. Maintaining position in one spot against tide or wind but not making progress in any direction.

STEP. *See* Mast Step.

STERN. The rear of a boat.

STERN BEARING. A simple friction type bearing placed on a propellor shaft at the opposite end to the stuffing box.

STERN FRAME. The frame around the inside of the transom.

STERN LIGHT. A shrouded light fixed at the stern. *See* Navigation Lights *illustration.*

STERNPOST. A stout upright timber at the stern.

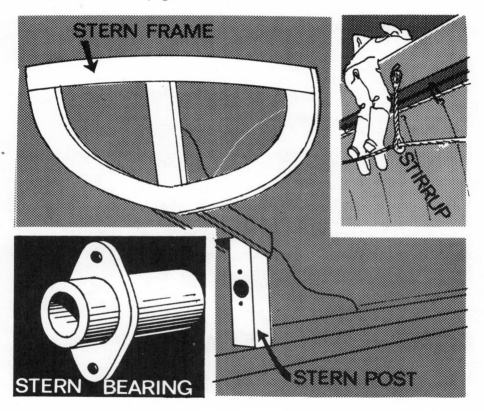

STERN TUBE. The correct name for 'propellor tube'. *See* Propellor Tube.

STERNWAY. Astern motion of vessel.

STIFF. Said of a vessel that stands up well in a blow.

STIRRUP. The rope lanyards from the yard which carry the footrope.

STOCK. The bar which prevents an anchor rolling over and losing its grip. *See* Admiralty Pattern Anchor.

STOCKLESS ANCHOR. One having no cross-bar such as the Dreadnought and Plough.

STOCKS. The erection which supports a ship during her building.

STONE BOAT. A nickname for a ferro-cement boat.

STOPPER. A short length of rope used to 'stop' a larger rope or cable temporarily. The rolling hitch is ideal here as shown.

STOPPING. To 'stop' a seam is to prevent a leak by puttying or caulking.

STOPS. Short lengths of line kept handy for securing small articles around the deck.

STORM. Winds of 56 to 63 knots. Force II on the Beaufort Scale.

STORM BOUND. Confined to port because of bad weather. Also called 'weather bound'.

STORM SAILS. Heavily made sails for use in extreme weather conditions. With the advent of synthetic sails these have become almost obsolete, a reefed synthetic sail being able to handle most conditions.

STOVE IN. When the sides or bottom have been smashed in the hull is said to be 'stove in'.

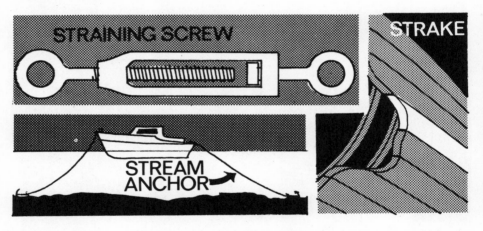

STOW. To pack articles aboard in such a manner that they will remain in place regardless of sea conditions.

STRAINING SCREW. A type of rigging screw having a swivel hook at one end and a threaded part at the other.

STRAKE. A hull plank.

STRAPPED IN. Said of a vessel hard on the wind with the sheets in as far as they will go.

STREAM ANCHOR. One used to anchor the stern when fore and aft anchoring or for general kedging work.

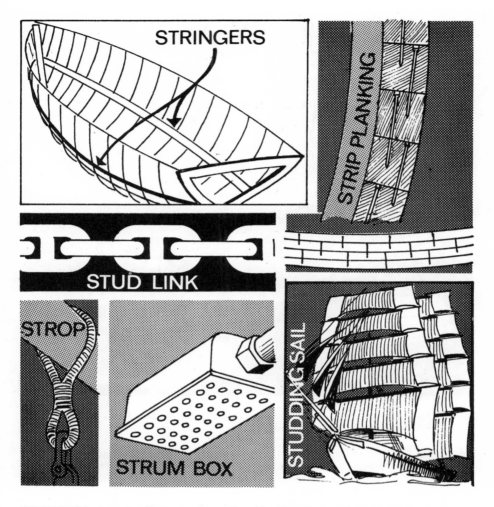

STRINGERS. Longitudinal members. Specifically refers to the members which fit inside the ribs of a timber hull imparting strength and integrity.

STRIP PLANKING. A method of timber construction where each plank, or strake, is edge nailed into the previous plank. The method produces a homogenous hull but is tedious to build. The planks can be either glued or painted between.

STRONG BREEZE. A wind of 22 to 27 knots. Force 6 in the Beaufort Scale.

STROP. A ring of rope around a spar to which blocks, etc. may be shackled.

STRUM BOX. A perforated metal box which acts as a sieve when placed over the end of a suction line. For example, the bilge pump inlet.

STUDDING SAIL. Light weather sails attached to either side of a square sail between studding sail booms. Also called 'stunsails'.

STUD LINK. A chain link strengthened against stretch by a stud across the widest part.

STUFFING BOX. As shown in the illustration opposite, this is a shaft
  bearing which also prevents water from entering the hull via the
  propellor tube. The gland is packed with greasy hemp or a modern
  synthetic and held in a compressed state by the gland housing.
  A stuffing box can be placed either internally and externally or at
  only one end of the shaft. If only one is used the other end of the
  shaft is born by a similar fitting, minus the stuffing gland, simply called
  a 'stern bearing'. The term 'stuffing box' can be applied to any bearing
  which prohibits the entrance of liquid or air.

SUMLOG. Probably derived from the words, 'submerged log', a speed and
  distance instrument with the impellor protruding from the bottom of
  the vessel which transmits to an information head via a flexible cable.
  A more recent type operates electrically having a pressure switch
  outside the hull. The increasing pressure caused by the speed of the
  vessel is interpreted at the head into speed and distance.

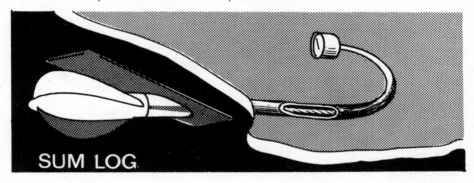

SUN SIGHTS. Altitudes of the sun (angle between it and the earth's horizon)
  taken by sextant.

SUPERCARGO. Man carried aboard ship to supervise the loading and
  unloading of cargo. Now redundant, his work mostly being done by the
  First Mate. During the changeover to all black crews on the North
  Australian Pearling Luggers, a white supervisor was carried and was
  known as the 'supercargo' or 'white engineer'.

SUPERCHARGER. A device for forcing more air into an engine than it
  would normally breathe to increase compression and rate of firing.
  Most commonly used on high speed diesel engines to achieve maximum
  output and minimum weight. Supercharged engines are often called
  'blown engines'.

SWAGE. A method of attaching an eye or jaw to the end of rigging wire
  without splicing or turning the wire back on itself in any way.
  A tube slightly larger than the wire's diameter is placed over the end
  then compressed over the wire under great pressure by machine.

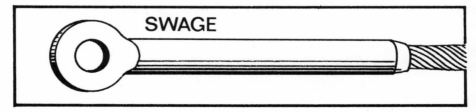

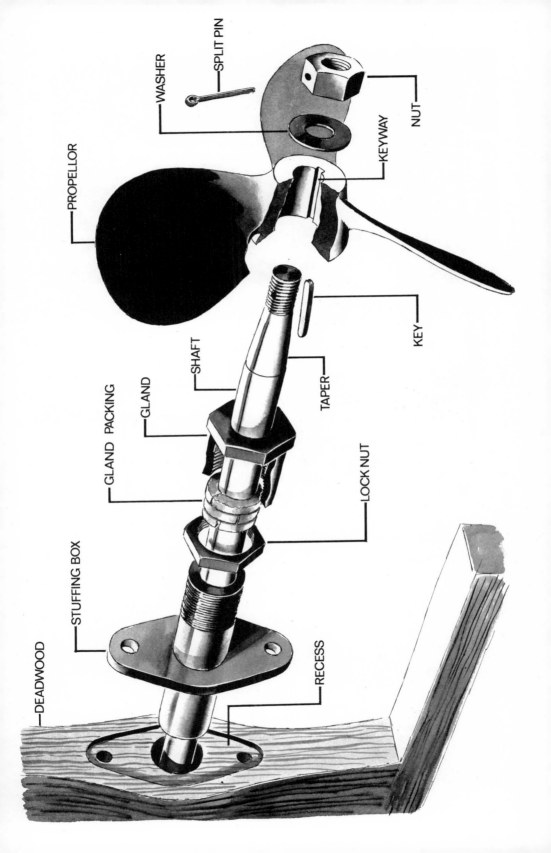

WASHER

SPLIT PIN

NUT

KEYWAY

PROPELLOR

KEY

SHAFT

GLAND

TAPER

GLAND PACKING

LOCK NUT

STUFFING BOX

DEADWOOD

RECESS

SWALLOW. The opening in a block through which a rope is rove.
See Common Block *illustration*.

SWELL. Long unbroken waves caused by meteorological conditions
in another area.

SWIG. To sweat rope in by pulling out at right angles and quickly letting go.
The rope thus captured is trapped with a half turn around a cleat.

SWINGING THE COMPASS. Also called 'swinging ship', this is a means of
determining the compass error before leaving port. The vessel is anchored
or moored at a known point and slowly swung through 360 degrees.
Every ten degrees (at least) a bearing is taken from a common object.
This is later compared with the known bearing and the difference is the
compass error on that heading.

SWIVEL. A fully rotating fitting placed in cables which experience a
constant turning action. For example, a swivel should be placed in a
mooring cable to prevent it winding itself short.

SWIVEL BLOCK. A block of any kind with a swivel incorporated into
its design.

SYNTACTIC FOAM. Small synthetic bubbles, or balloons, used to make a
putty with the addition of polyester or epoxy resin. These are known
as 'microballoons'.

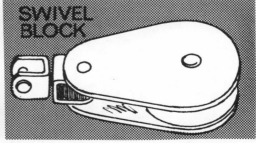

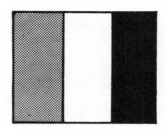

T. Flag of the International Code of Signals meaning, 'Keep clear of me; I am engaged in pair trawling'. Coloured red, white and blue in vertical stripes.

TABERNACLE. Any steel or timber frame used to support the foot of the mast. More commonly used to describe a fitting which allows the mast to hinge down.

TABLING. The strengthened hem of a sail to which the bolt rope is sewn.

TACHOMETER. Instrument for recording the revolutions of an engine. Also records hours run.

TACK. The lower forward corner of a fore and aft sail. 2. The course of a sailing vessel stated in relation to the wind. Thus, port or starboard tack.

TACKLE. A general term for all the running rigging aboard a sailing vessel. Specifically refers to a combination of rope and blocks.

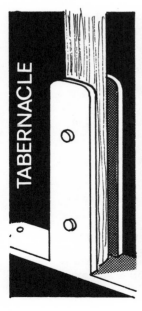
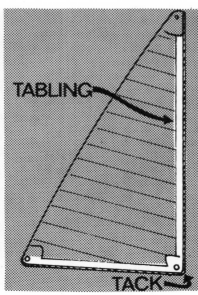
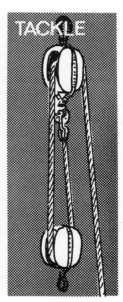

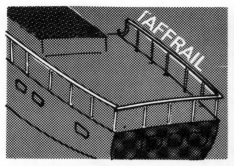

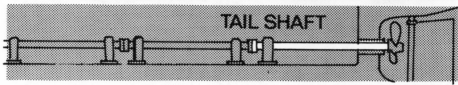

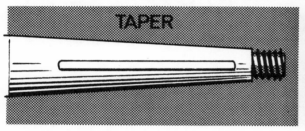

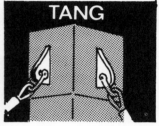

TAFFRAIL. The timber rail around the stern deck of a vessel. Usually protects a poop deck area only.

TAIL BOARD. The ornamental carved boards extending under the bow from beneath the bowsprit. Sometimes called 'trail boards'.

TAIL SHAFT. Alternative name for propellor shaft. In big ships refers to the after-most section of a multi section shaft.

TAKE A TURN. To put a turn of rope or cable onto a bitt to temporarily take the strain prior to bringing in more slack and finally making fast.

TAKE IN. To lower sails. To haul in.

TAKE UP. After drying out, the swelling of planks after being placed in water. The seams 'take up' and become watertight.

TANG. The part of a mast band, shroud hoop, mast cap, etc., which takes the shroud or stay end.

TAPER. The tapered end of a shaft over which a propellor or coupling fits. The standard taper for a propellor is one in 16 as shown.

TAR EPOXY. A mixture of tar and epoxy resin used in the treatment of bare steel. It is best applied direct to bright steelwork to an even thickness and in a warm state. Before the application of ordinary paints the wax which rises to the surface must be sanded back, otherwise silver paint can be applied to the epoxy before it hardens.

TEE BOLLARD. A 'T' shaped bollard as shown.

TEE CLEAT. A 'T' shaped cleat as shown.

TELLTALE. An indicator showing the angle of rudder to the helmsman; the speed and direction of engines to an engineer; or the wind direction to the sailing man. The latter consists of a small flag fixed top and one side to a metal frame (as illustrated) and is also known as a 'bandrol'.

TELLTALE COMPASS. An upside-down compass fitted to the deckhead above a bunk so that the master or navigator can ascertain the course without turning out.

TENDER. The dinghy. Any small boat used to attend the mother ship.

TEREDO. *See* Ship Worm. Correct name 'teredo navalis'.

TERYLENE. Trade name in Australia for a product of polyester resin. American name 'Dacron'. *See* Polyester.

THAMES BARGE. A shallow draught, ketch or yawl rigged barge-yacht used on the Thames River.

TEE BOLLARD

TEE CLEAT

TELL TALE

THAMES BARGE

THERMAL EQUATOR. The 'hot belt' which closely follows the true equator.

THERMOPLASTIC. A plastic which can be softened by heat after which it will harden back to its original form.

THERMOSETTING. A plastic which cannot be changed in character after setting without destroying its properties.

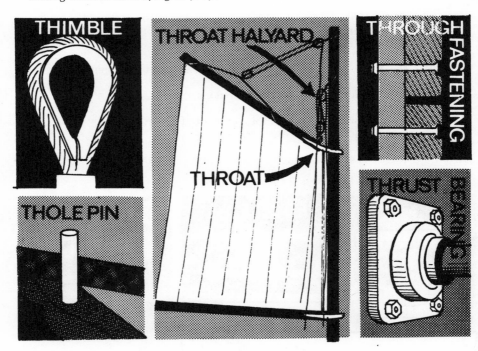

THIMBLE. A round or heart shaped metal eye with a concave groove around the edge to take rope or wire.

THIXOTROPIC RESIN. A resin which does not run of its own accord yet will readily brush out. Ideal for vertical surfaces.

THOLE PIN. A wooden peg stood vertically in the gunwhale of a boat against which the oar rests.

THROAT. The fore upper corner of a gaff mainsail where the gaff boom touches the mast.

THROAT HALYARD. The tackles used to hoist the throat end of the gaff aloft.

THROUGH FASTENINGS. Any fastening that passes right through the objects and is secured on both ends (such as a bolt and nut or a copper nail and roove).

THRUST BEARING. A bearing designed to support a shaft in a normal way whilst resisting fore and aft thrust. The shaft must have a flange which prevents it pushing through the thrust bearing as shown.

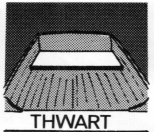

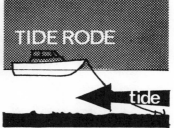

THUMB CLEAT. A one horned cleat used mainly as a fairlead. Small types are ideal as lashing points for awnings, dodgers, etc.

THWART. A transverse seat in a rowing boat.

TIDAL HARBOUR. A harbour which admits vessels only at a certain stage of tide.

TIDE. The rise and fall of the sea due to centrifugal force of the earth's rotation and the gravitational pull of the sun and moon.

TIDE RODE. Said of an anchored or moored vessel when her bow is lying towards the current.

TILLER. A lever fitted directly into the rudder head and used as a steering device.

TILLER EXTENSION. A free swivelling rod attached to the tiller to permit the helmsman greater scope in his movements. Ideal in skiffs where the helmsman may be called upon to lean out with the rest of the crew.

TILLER EXTENSION UNIVERSAL. The coupling between tiller and tiller extension.

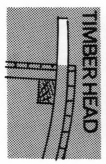

TIMBER HITCH

TIMBERHEADS. Vertical timbers projecting above deck used for making fast. Specifically refers to ends of ribs which continue above deck.

TIMBER HITCH. A hitch used when towing a spar or log as shown.

TINGLE. A temporary patch of copper, plywood or lead placed over a leak. It should be fastened down on painted canvas or caulking compound.

TOE RAIL. The full length raised part around the gunwhale to prevent crew from slipping off the deck. Might be thought of as a very low 'bulwark'.

TOE RAIL CAPPING. The ornamental strip laid along the top of the toe rail. Usually varnished.

TOE STRAPS. The webbing running fore and aft along the bottom of a sailing skiff under which the crew place their feet when leaning out.

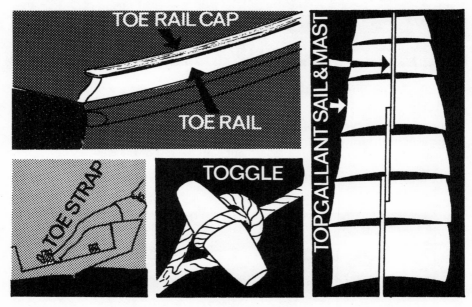

TOGGLE. A short tapered piece of hardwood held at the centre by a lanyard. Passed through an eye, two lengths of line are united. A modern form of toggle is used extensively in rigging screw attachment. The principle is also used in quick action pins.

TOPGALLANT MAST. The third mast from the deck.

TOPGALLANT SAIL. The sail set above the topsail.

TOPMAST. The second mast from the deck. *See* Topgallant Mast *illustration.*

TOPPING LIFT. The tackles used to hoist a derrick or any type of boom.

TOPSAIL. A sail set above the mainsail in fore and aft rigs and above the course in square rigged ships.

TOPSAIL SCHOONER. A normal schooner rigged vessel carrying squaresails on the foremast.

TOP SIDES. The area of hull between waterline and gunwhale.

TOP TIMBER. The timber above the futtocks. *See* Futtocks *illustration.*

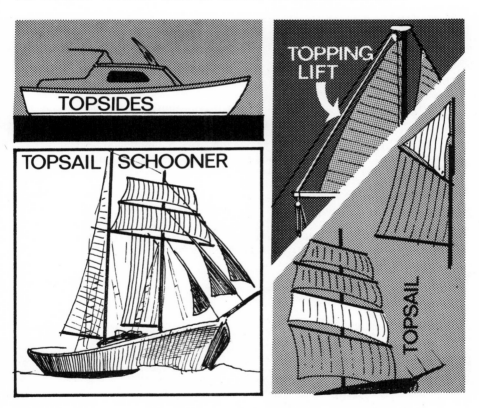

TRACK. The course of the vessel. 2. Any device used to guide and restrain its host. For example, mainsail track holds the slides in place; jib sheet track permits infinite adjustment to the sheeting angle.

TRACK SLIDES. Any device made to fit and run in a track system. There are various types from the old male brass track with female brass slides to the modern aluminium female track and male nylon slides. Various types are shown under the heading Sail Track.

TRADE WINDS. A belt of constant winds around the earth's surface blowing from a high pressure system into the equatorial low pressure and curved towards the west by the earth's rotation. Generally speaking the winds blow south-east between 10 to 20 degrees latitude in the southern hemisphere and north-east between similar parallels in the northern hemisphere. *See* Weather.

TRAIL BOARDS. Ornamental boards along the ship's sides near the stern. The term is often used to denote the decorative strips behind the bowsprit which are, in fact, called 'tail boards'. The term 'trail boards' might properly describe decorative boards immediately behind a figure head, however.

TRAILER-SAILER. A small yacht of maximum beam and minimum draught which is hauled out of the water and carried from place to place on a trailer. These boats are mostly centreboarders and tend to have a maximum length of 6.5 metres (about 22 feet).

TRAINING WALLS. Those embankments placed in a river or channel to 'train' the waterway to maintain a constant direction. A scouring action also tends to maintain constant depth. Training walls are very common close to the mouth of a large river. A typical arrangement of walls is shown in the illustration.

TRANSIT. The line between the observer and two objects when those objects are in line.

TRANSOM. The 'back' of the hull.

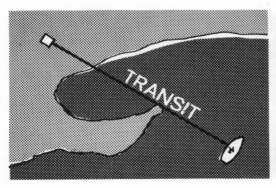

TRANSOM HANDLE. A cast metal fitting used as a handle when carrying small boats.

TRANSOM STERN. The description of a vessel having a transom type stern as against one having a counter stern or cruiser stern, etc.

TRAPEZE. A device used in sailing skiffs to gain maximum leverage and thus maximum righting moment. A crewman hangs out from a 'trapeze' which is a wire rope from the mast to a harness which fits the waist.

TRAPEZE RING. The fitting which unites the supporting rope with the body harness whilst also providing a handhold.

TRAVELLER. *See* Mainsheet Traveller.

TRAWLER. A vessel designed to fish by use of a net towed astern. Usually of high power and maximum buoyancy aft of amidships.

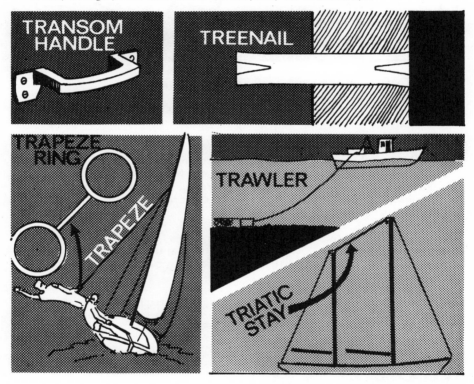

TREENAIL. (Often pronounced 'trennel'). A method of securing planks to a frame in boatbuilding. The 'nail' is of timber and is held in place by a wedge. Modern methods have antiquated treenail fastening, however the system still has a place in deck construction where a laid deck is used. The all-timber components wear evenly instead of leaving rises where fastenings are placed.

TRESTLE TREES. The fore and aft members of a lower and upper mast union. Details are shown under 'Cross Trees'.

TRIATIC STAY. The stay connecting two masts together.

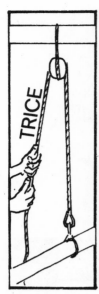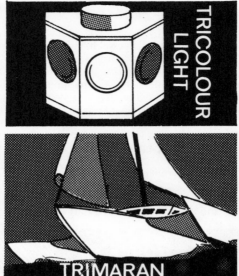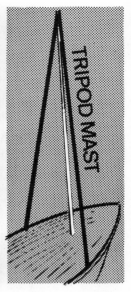

TRICE. To haul something up by pulling down on tackle.

TRICOLOUR LIGHT. A combination navigation light having red, white and green lights. Permissible on small boats but illegal on commercial shipping of any type.

TRIMARAN. A three hull, unballasted vessel depending on the buoyancy of the leeward hull for stability. This type became very popular during the 1960's with the advent of modern glues, fibreglass and plywood coupled with the belief that they were much cheaper to construct than conventional craft.

TRIPOD MAST. A three part mast requiring no stays. The three parts form a triangle at the base and 'lean' against each other at the top where they unite. Has been tried in modern experimental craft, but the idea dates to ancient times.

TROCHOIDAL DRIVE. An arrangement used in craft requiring high manoeuvrability where the propellor is fully swivelling so that it can be used as a rudder as well as a drive unit.

TROCHOIDAL WAVE. A sea wave of orderly movement and shape.

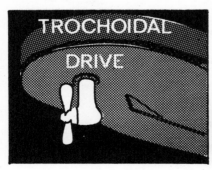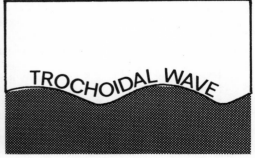

TROUGH. The hollow between two waves.

TRUCK. Round piece of wood used to cap a mast. Mostly used on flag poles.

TRUSS FRAME. A web frame used in ferro-cement construction. According to designer's recommendations, the frame can be established first or the hull can be built over a sacrificial structure and the truss frames knitted in later during construction.

TRYSAIL. A small sail used during bad weather in place of the mainsail.

TUCK. After part of a hull where it rises to become the counter.

TUBULAR JAMB CLEAT. As shown, a jamb cleat which also acts as a lead.

TULARIT SPLICE. A soft metal collar which is clamped by mechanical press around wire to form an eye.

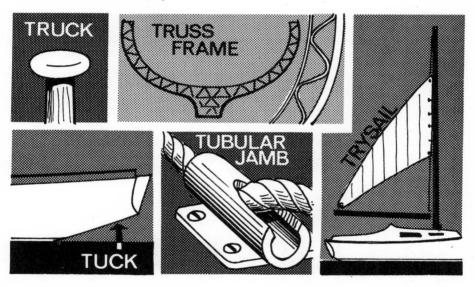

TUMBLE HOME. Where the deck is of less beam than the widest part of the hull the inclination of the topsides into the deck is called the 'tumble home'.

TUMBLER. The pivoted 'shoe' trapped within a gaff's jaw to hold the gaff away from the mast and to help it run true.

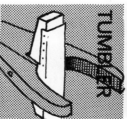

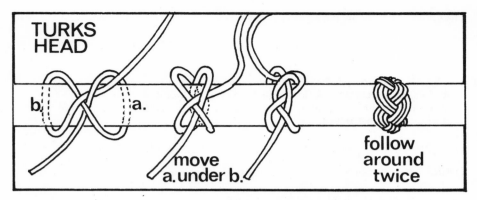

TURKS
HEAD

b. a.

move
a. under b.

follow
around
twice

TURKS HEAD. This is one of the most commonly used knots in decorative work. It is best formed around a cylinder and can be made in three parts, four parts, etc., until it completely covers the object. The three part turks head is illustrated.

TURN BUCKLE. Alternative name for rigging screw, bottle screw, etc.

TURN BUTTON. A simple device used to hold locker doors, drawers, etc. closed.

TWIN BACKSTAYS. Two individual backstays used to support a mast. Run from the masthead to the stern of the boat.

TWIN SAILS. Identical headsails (jibs or genoas) set as illustrated for use when passage making with constant winds. Traditionally they replace the squaresail and have similar characteristics. Lines may be taken from the pole ends, back through blocks to the tiller to effect a self steering system.

TWIN UNION. Two derricks alongside each other used in harmony to load and unload cargo. The derricks are tied back in such a way that they hang outboard and cargo is hoisted and traversed between the two.

TURN BUTTON

TWIN HEADSAILS

TWIN BACKSTAYS

TWIN UNION

TWO BLOCKS. Same as 'chock-o-block' described under that heading.

TWO SHOT METHOD. In ferro-cement construction, where the hull is plastered half a thickness at a time, first from outside then from inside. Whereas it is ideal to plaster in one shot, or 'hit', the two shot method appears successful and takes the pressure off workmen who have more time to prevent voids and to apply a stronger mix because less water is required to make it penetrate. The first shot is allowed to cure then the other shot is applied over a fresh grout of cement-epoxy mix.

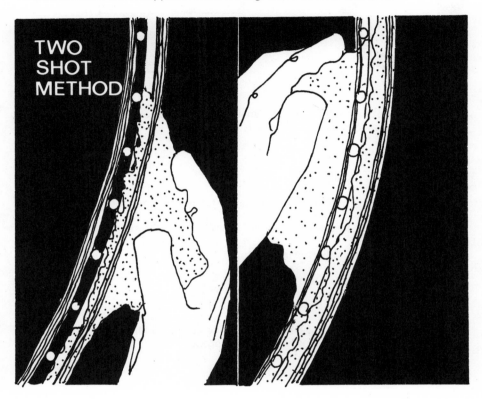

TWO
SHOT
METHOD

 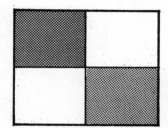

U. Flag of the International Code of Signals meaning, 'You are running into danger'. It is chequered white and red.

UNBEND. To untie.

UNDER CANVAS. Under sail.

UNDER CANVASSED. Carrying too little sail for prevailing conditions.

UNDERTOW. The seaward run of current from a surf or river entrance.

UNFURL. To free the sails preparatory to hoisting.

UNION PURCHASE. *See* Twin Union.

UNSHIP. To remove from the vessel. To lift a mast out, for example.

UREA FORMALDEHYDE GLUE. A useful glue in boatbuilding for internal fitting out. Is water resistant but not waterproof.

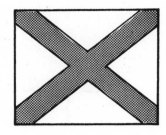

V. Flag of the International Code of Signals meaning, 'I require assistance'. A red diagonal cross on a white background.

VACUUM TOILET. A recently developed system for the elimination of human waste out of a boat from below the waterline. The toilet bowl itself is placed in the vacuum line of a simple pump. By closing the lid, which seals onto the bowl, waste matter within is drawn out when pumped. An air valve on the inlet side of the line releases the lid when the operation is complete. This last step is important to avoid accidental sinking of the vessel. Unless released a syphoning effect can occur with the overflow weeping into the boat from under the toilet lid, despite its seal.

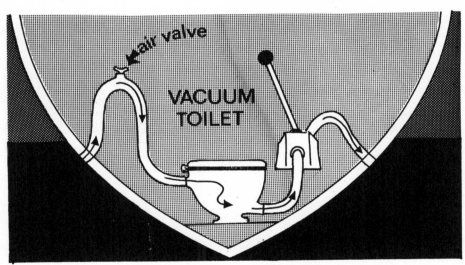

VANE STEERING. A method of making a sailing boat steer herself by the action of a vernier rudder attached to the main rudder. The vernier rudder is actuated by a wind vane. There are many variations to the theme. A most basic method is illustrated.

VANG. A rope rigged to the end of the gaff to prevent it sagging to leeward.

VARIATION. The angle between true north and magnetic north caused by the natural magnetic movement of the earth's poles.

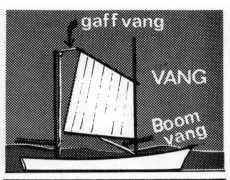

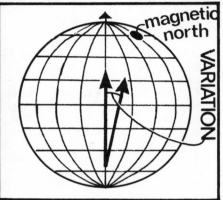

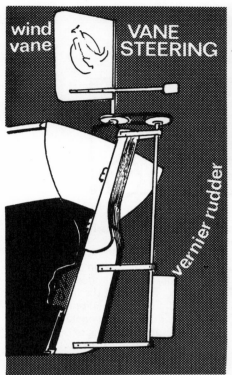

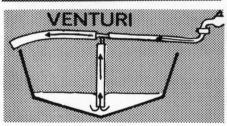

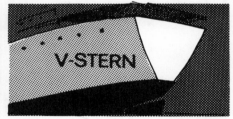

VEER. To pay out rope or cable. 2. When the wind alters direction clockwise.

VENTILATOR. Any device which admits fresh air below decks and eliminates foul air. *See* Cowl Ventilator, Mushroom Ventilator, etc.

VENTURI. A pumping system utilising the natural force of passing water.

VERNIER. *See* Sextant *illustration.*

VERY'S LIGHTS. Distress signals showing red, white or green stars fired from a pistol.

VESSEL. An overall description for any and every type of boat, ship, yacht, launch, etc.

V-STERN. An almost vertical, 'V' shaped transom. Common on modern ships.

Left: *Except for the few remaining ships around the world, the day of square rig is dead. The future fuel crisis might yet cause their rebirth, probably with aluminium masts and electronically controlled sails.*

Above: *A slipway, or marine railway, consists of a cradle in which sits the vessel, and two or more steel tracks extending underwater for a few metres. A winch hauls the cradle onto dry land.*

Below: *This horrific contraption requires about six crewmen to operate it and threatens life and limb as the chain tries to slip on its drum. It is an anchor winch on a North Australian Pearling Lugger and has remained unchanged for decades.*

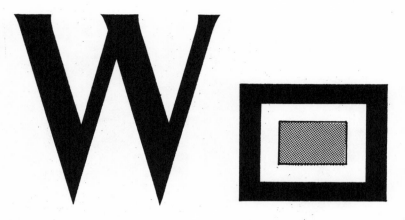

W. Flag of the International Code of Signals meaning, 'I require medical assistance'. Coloured blue, white and red.

WAD PUNCH. A punch used for making holes in leather, canvas, synthetic material to receive a metal eyelet.

WAIST. The deck between the forecastle and poop. If not thus defined can be used to describe the general area of a vessel where the sides tend to parallel each other.

WAKE. The disturbed water behind a vessel under way.

WALE. The thickest strake in a timber ship. Usually the one above the waterline where it is known as a 'bend'. *See* Bends *illustration.*

WALL KNOT. As illustrated, a knot made in the end of a rope by unlaying the strands then passing each one through the bight of its neighbour.

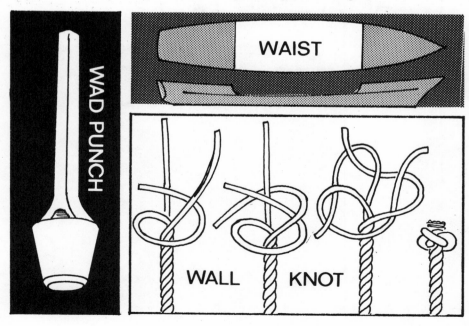

WALL SIDED. Said of a vessel having high, flat sides. Also called 'slab sided'.

WALTHER ENGINE. A propulsion unit designed by Hellmuth Walther in 1933 to be used in submarines with the aim of continued running without natural oxygen. Hydrogen peroxide was broken down by a chemical catalyst into water and oxygen. The liberated oxygen was fed into a combustion chamber with diesel fuel. Water injected into the chamber became high pressure steam which was then directed into a steam turbine engine. Thus a submarine could remain underwater carrying its own oxygen in its fuel supply. Late in World War II, Hitler ordered 100 subs powered by Walther engines, but too late to change the course of the war. Soon after, nuclear power obsoleted the idea entirely.

WANING. Said of the moon when in its third and fourth quarters and the illumination is decreasing.

WARP. To move a vessel from one place to another by the use of ropes (warps).

WASH STRAKE. The upper strake in a ship's topsides. Also called 'sheer strake'.

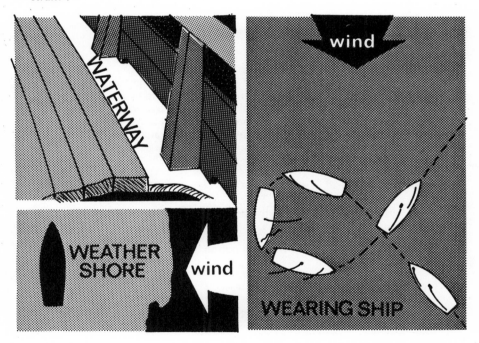

WATERWAYS. Channels along the edge of the deck which carry water to the scuppers. Also name of structural member. *See* Margin Plank *illustration.*

WEARING SHIP. Going from one tack to another by turning the ship's stern through the wind. Sometimes called 'doing an old man'.

WEATHER SHORE. A shore that is to windward of a vessel. If the vessel moves in close she would be under the lee of that coastline which is a protected situation.

WEATHER. The phenomena within the earth's atmosphere caused by ascending and descending currents over hot and cold regions respectively plus the rotation of the earth. The illustration opposite shows these basic vertical currents. It can be seen that high pressure occurs under descending air and low pressure occurs under ascending air. Horizontal movement is given to these currents, turning them into winds, by the earth's rotation and the fact that wind tends to blow clockwise around low pressure and anti-clockwise around high pressure in the southern hemisphere (the opposite occurs in the northern hemisphere).

WEATHER SIDE. The side on which the wind blows.

WEB FRAMES. *See* Truss Frames.

WEDGE TYPE HULL. A modern type of sailing hull with the greatest buoyancy aft of amidships. It has a fine entry (bow) and excessively buoyant stern sections giving its waterline plane a 'wedge' shape. This wedge shape helps the hull claw to windward when tacking. The type also automatically lends itself to excessive beam-shallow draught, which, coupled with a short, deep fin keel, also helps in windward efficiency. *See* Heeled Waterlines *for more details.*

WEFT. The lateral thread in woven material.

WEIGH. To lift anchor. 'Weigh Anchor' means to lift anchor and get under way.

WEST COUNTRY WHIPPING. Whipping put on by a succession of overhand knots. It is finished with a reef knot.

WESTING. Making a good course to the west.

WETTED SURFACE. The area of a hull that is in contact with the water.

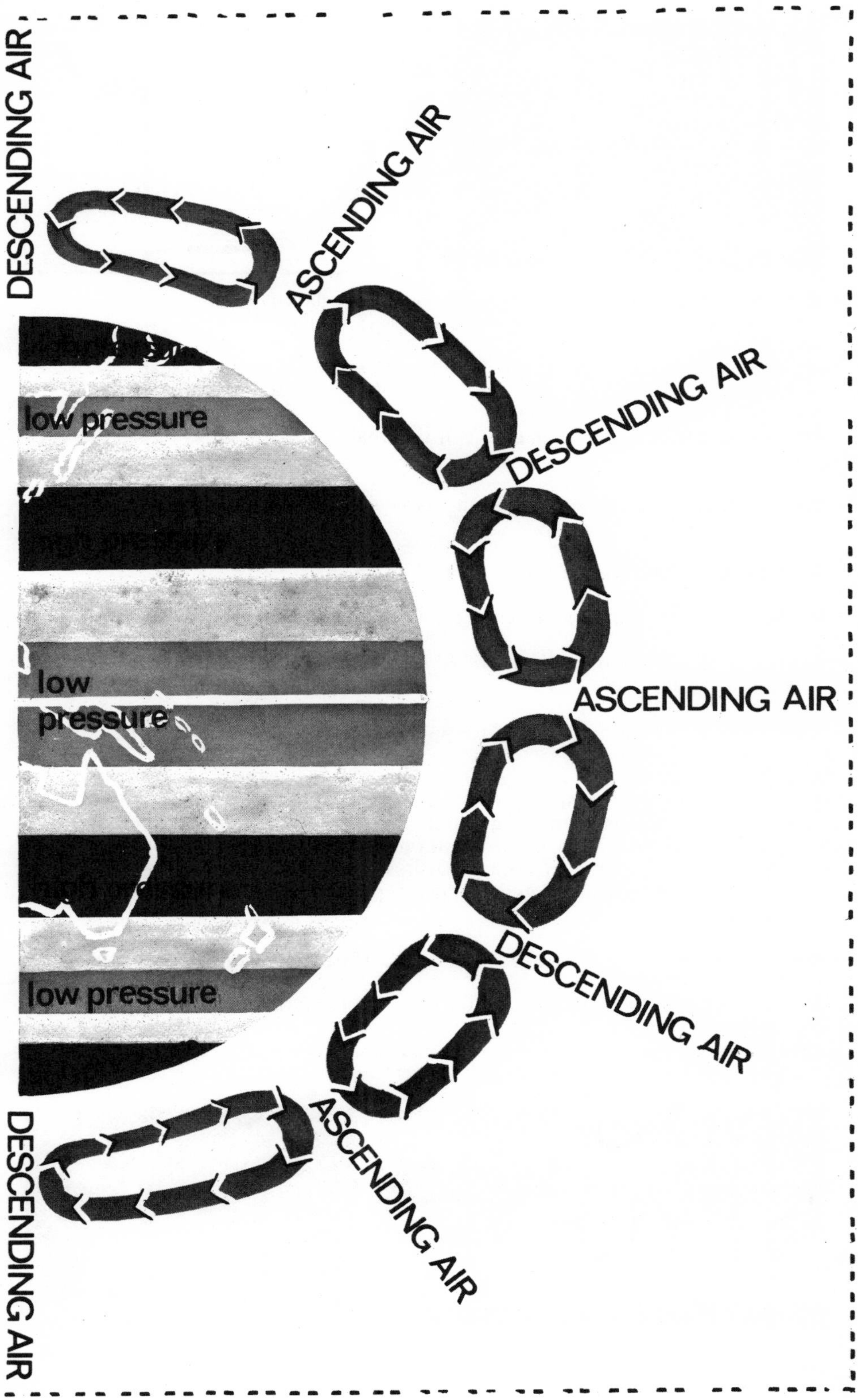

DESCENDING AIR

ASCENDING AIR

DESCENDING AIR

ASCENDING AIR

DESCENDING AIR

ASCENDING AIR

DESCENDING AIR

low pressure

low pressure

low pressure

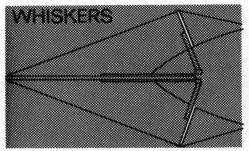

WETTING OUT. Bringing the resin up through fibreglass by rolling across the mat with ridged rollers whilst the resin is still wet.

WHARF. Any erection against the shore for ships to lie alongside to load and discharge cargo, passengers, etc. Also called pier, jetty and dock.

WHARFINGER. The person in charge of the wharf. Also known as 'piermaster'.

WHISKERS. 'Spreaders' projecting out from near the catheads to spread the jib-boom shrouds or guys.

WHITE CAPS. Foam on the top of waves.

WHITE HORSES. Fast running white caps.

WHOLE GALE. Wind of a velocity of 48 to 55 knots. Force 10 of the Beaufort Scale.

WIDE DEE SHACKLES. A common shackle with wider jaws than usual.

WINCH. A device used for hauling in ropes or chain and giving the operator a leverage factor dependent on the job. Some winches have variable ratios which can be selected by moving a lever whilst more sophisticated types have automatic gear changes dependent on the loadings. The three main types in use aboard ship are anchor winch, sheet winch and halyard winch. The illustration opposite shows a popular type of sheet winch in exploded view.

WINDJAMMER. Nickname for a sailing vessel. Usually applied to large vessels.

WIND RODE. Said of a vessel at anchor when she lies bow to wind.

WIND SAIL. A specially shaped piece of canvas which sets above a hatch and directs wind down and into the vessel.

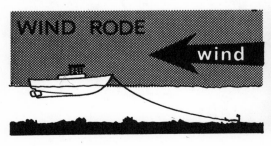

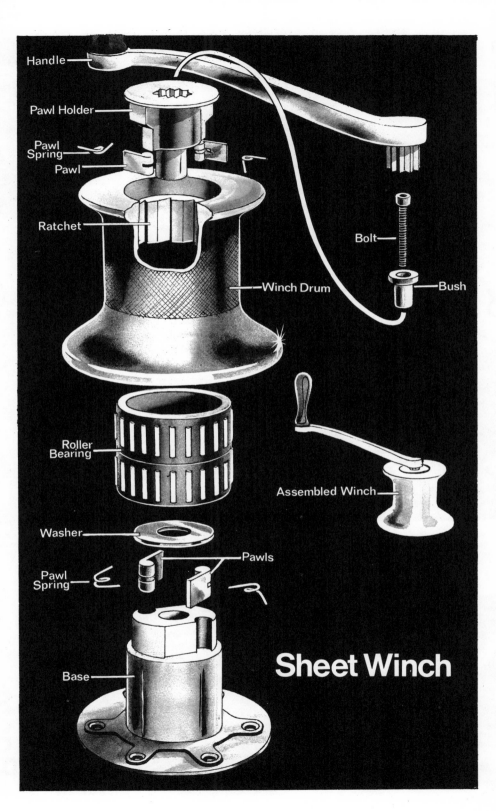

Handle

Pawl Holder

Pawl
Spring

Pawl

Ratchet

Bolt

Bush

Winch Drum

Roller
Bearing

Assembled Winch

Washer

Pawls

Pawl
Spring

Base

Sheet Winch

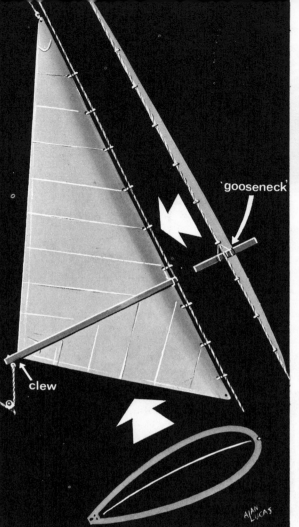

'gooseneck'

clew

A wishbone boomed sail must be cut to fit entirely within the boom (above) and not be so slack as to easily lie against same. This type of boom is very well behaved having no tendency to rise and fall. A small boom can be constructed as shown below. The sides are laminated timber with the leading end, or 'gooseneck', fitted so that it will swivel against the stay yet not fall away.

The 'gooseneck' (top) can be held against the stay by this simple method if the wishbone boom is small. Ideally a long, vertical shoe should be incorporated. The photograph (above) shows the wishbone under working conditions. One of its greatest advantages is the single-point sheeting system.
It requires no vang or other apparatus to make it behave.

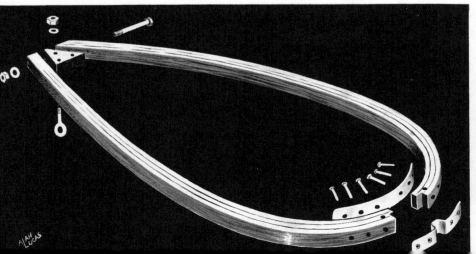

Wishbone Boom

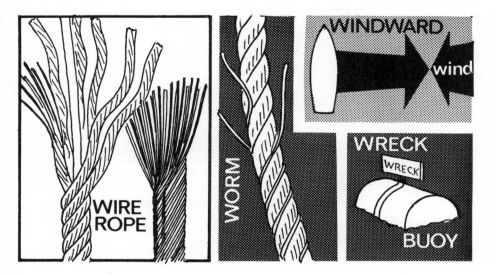

WIND VANE. *See* Vane Steering.

WINDWARD. Towards the wind.

WING AND WING. Said of a vessel sailing with twin headsail or with main out one side and mizzen out the opposite side. Also called 'goosewinged'.

WIRE ROPE. Made of stainless steel, plain steel or plain steel galvanised, wire rope is usually made up of a number of wires laid left handed into a strand then a number of strands (usually six) are laid right handed around a heart into the finished rope. Depending on the number of wires in a strand the rope is either flexible or non flexible and is used in either running rigging or standing rigging respectively. Any wire rope of under 19 wires per strand must not be used through a block.

WISHBONE BOOM. A two sided boom which embraces the sail from the luff to the clew. Because a triangle of sail lies below the boom it cannot lift and as a result greater instant efficiency is enjoyed. This advantage is most appreciated when running square at which time club booms have the tendency to rise and flop and sometimes try to pass forward of the stay and turn the sail 'inside out'. The wishbone boom cannot do this. It is consequently a safer, less worrying type. The illustration shows a simple form of wishbone. More sophisticated methods of attachment to the luff and stay should be employed in large craft or those vessels employing more than one wishbone boom.

WISHBONE RIG. A vessel whose rig is designed to take advantage of wishbone booms forward of the aft mast. Whilst they have all the advantages mentioned under 'Wishbone Boom', the all-wishbone rig does present a problem of furling. Also, booms aloft can cause considerable wear and damage in a seaway with little wind.

WORM. To fill the spaces (or cantlines) between the strands of a rope before parcelling and serving. Any type of small stuff can be used. *See* Serving.

WRECK BUOY. A green painted buoy with the word 'wreck' plainly visible placed over the site of a known wreck to warn mariners away.

X.   Flag of the International Code of Signals meaning, 'Stop carrying out
     your intentions and watch for my signals'. A white blackground with
     blue cross.

Y. Flag of the International Code of Signals meaning, 'I am dragging my anchor'. Yellow and red diagonal stripes.

YACHT. Of Dutch derivation, a private vessel be she power or sail, but most commonly used to denote a sailing vessel.

YANKEE. A jib topsail commonly used on cutters, ketches and schooners.

YARD. Spar fitted athwartships from which hangs the squaresail. These sails are named in the front of this book on illustrations of various sailing ship types.

YARD ARM. That part of the yard lying outside the lift.

YARN. The parts of a strand of rope.

YAWL. A two masted sailing boat with the mizzen mast aft of the rudder.

YOKE. A fitting over the rudder head to which lines are attached instead of a tiller.

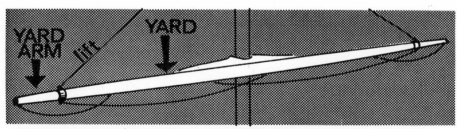

 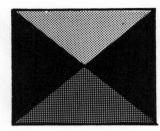

Z. Flag of the International Code of Signals meaning, 'I require a tug'. When made by fishing vessels operating in close proximity to fishing grounds it means, 'I am shooting nets'. Coloured black, yellow, blue and red as shown.

ZENITH. Point in the heavens directly above the observer.

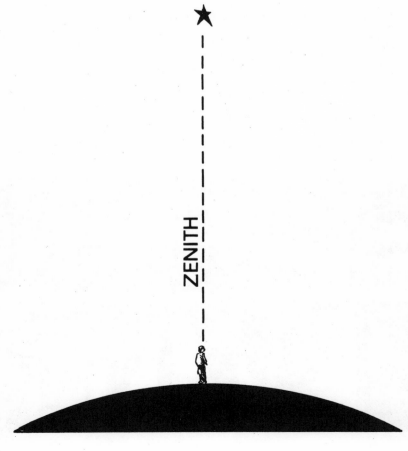